PENCIL ME IN

*The Business Drawing Book for
People Who Can't Draw*

BY CHRISTINA WODTKE

Pencil Me In: The Business Drawing Book Who Can't Draw

© 2017 Christina Wodtke

ISBN 0-9960060-3-6

Designed by Michel Vrana / michelvrana.com

Published by Christina Wodtke / pencilmeinthebook.com

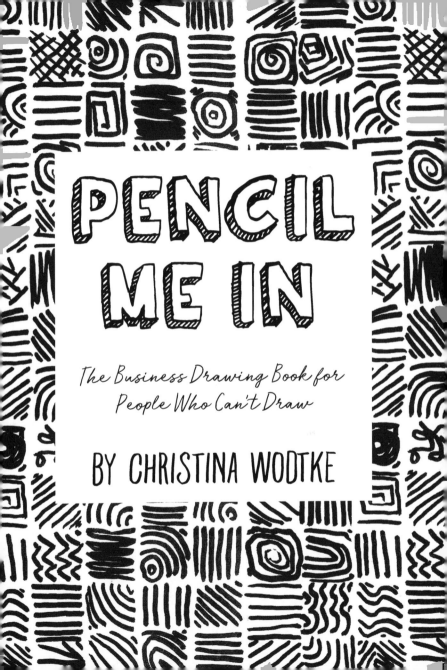

PENCIL ME IN

The Business Drawing Book for People Who Can't Draw

BY CHRISTINA WODTKE

WITH
CONTRIBUTIONS FROM

Amelie Sarrazin, Aleksandra Micek,
Taylor Reese, Dan Brown, Daniel Cook,
Kate Rutter, Eva-Lotta Lamm,
Matthew Magain, Sunni Brown,
Cristina Negrut, Daryl Meier Fahrni,
Marc Bourguignon, Laura Klein, David Gray,
Melissa Kim, Jherin Miller, Mike Rohde,
Brian Gulassa, Andrew Reid, Rolf Faste,
Raph Koster, Stone Librande, Robin Hunicke,
Alicia Loring, Erin Malone, Stephen P. Anderson,
Giorgia Lupi, Alex Osterwalder, Noelle Stransky,
James Young, and Dan Roam

and examples from scientists, architects, chefs,
architects, best-selling authors
and more....

DEDICATION

For the students of California College of the Arts, Stanford Continuing Studies and my many workshops who kept asking for this book.

For my amazing beta-readers, who were generous with their time and feedback.

But mostly for my daughter Amelie, who drew with me, critiqued the pictures and the words, and astounds me every day with her insights and creativity. I love you, kitten.

CONTENTS

INTRODUCTION

While I was writing I kept thinking, "Who am I to make this book?"

I studied painting in Art School and went on to have a great career in fine dining. Frustrated and footsore, I taught myself HTML and got into "this new internet thing."

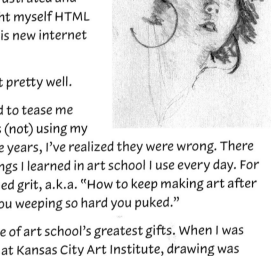

That worked out pretty well.

My parents used to tease me about how I was (not) using my degree. Over the years, I've realized they were wrong. There are so many things I learned in art school I use every day. For example, I learned grit, a.k.a. "How to keep making art after a critique had you weeping so hard you puked."

Drawing was one of art school's greatest gifts. When I was at Kansas City Art Institute, drawing was taught as a kind of Zen practice. You were taught that your idea of a face or a house got in the way of truly seeing it. You needed to stop thinking about what it was and relax into seeing what really was there.

For example, on the left is an idea of a house, the kind a kid draws. On the right is a house in my neighborhood. Houses rarely look like the one on the left.

When I started making websites in the '90s, I found plenty of use for drawing. I made concept models, site maps, wireframes, and more! But I made them with software rather than with a pen and paper.

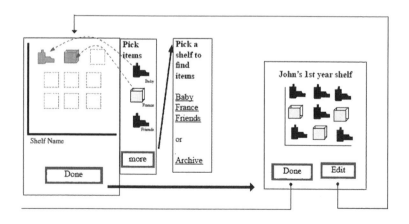

Much later, I realized that I was better off if I drew my ideas. I could explore a dozen ideas in the time it took me to open my software.

I drew at every company I worked with, from Yahoo to The New York Times. At tech companies, everyone draws on the whiteboard. When you make complex things, words eventually fail.

My sketches were pretty horrible. I knew how to draw things in the world, but not the things in my brain. I decided to learn how to draw ideas.

I could have kept drawing badly –you can make bad pictures and communicate a lot! But I wondered... if bad pictures communicated a lot, what could good pictures do? I filled a dozen sketchbooks exploring and practicing. As I became fluent in visual communication, it was like learning a new language. I could communicate complex ideas clearly and simply.

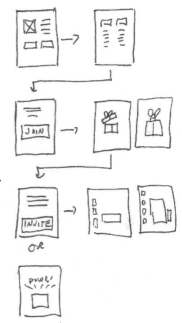

Me, Teaching, by Amelie, Age 8

Index card sketches by Aleksandra Micek, student at California College of the Arts

When I became a professor, I taught my students how to sketch ideas and model systems. One day a student came up to me and asked, "Is there a book on this kind of drawing?" All I could recommend was Ed Emberley's *Make a World*. It's a kid's book.

Where are the simple books on how to draw for grown-ups? Most books that teach drawing are intimidating. They teach you how to draw buildings or race cars or realistic people, but that's not what non-designers need to draw every day.

I decided to make a book for working professionals that wouldn't scare anyone away and would teach you how to draw the kinds of things you need to think through product and business decisions.

Here we are! **Let's draw!**

DRAWING, DRAFTING, AND DOODLING

People talk about drawing and sketching as if it's all the same kind of thing. But when I tried to draw my ideas, I struggled, even though I had studied painting.

I think there are three kinds of drawing (at least!).

Technically, an extinct bird drawing.

Life Drawing

The art of looking at the world and shutting up your verbal brain so you can draw what you see. The best book for this is Betty Edward's *Drawing on the Right Side of the Brain.*

Drafting

Used by architects and industrial designers, you use geometry and logic to render things as they eventually will appear in the world.

Idea Sketching (Also Called Doodling)

All about getting the stuff in your head out on the paper where you can see, evaluate, and share it.

This book is about that last kind.

EQUIPMENT

You will want a pencil, a pen and paper. I started with Sharpies and index cards. But Sharpies bleed through normal paper!

My favorite brands now are Micron and Tombow. If the pen's product description says, "archival ink," you won't get in trouble with fading (or accidently washing).

When I get a new set of pens, I always test each size, to see how I feel about the lines.

My first notebook was a Moleskine. They're in many stores, so they are easy to find. Now I use HandBook Travelogue and MUJI notebooks. MUJI are so cheap you feel good about making bad drawings! HandBook has the nicest paper, when you feel artsy.

My secret weapon is stencils. I love them for making geometric people.

A HISTORY OF MARK MAKING

We have been drawing for over 40,000 years. It's how we preserved our knowledge before writing.

Our brains have evolved to make and read pictures. So why do we stop drawing after the first grade?

Little children and early civilizations make the same marks. They all start with **handprints**.

Then we make **scribbles**, enjoying the pleasure of mark making for its own sake.

Handprint...   *and marks.*

Scribbles become **spirals** and **shapes**, and shapes are refined into **patterns**.

As we play, we discover new cool patterns we can make.

We graduate into drawing the things we see in the world. We can't help but include how we feel about the things we draw.

Finally, we start drawing our work life.

Petroglyphs from New Mexico, Arizona, Peru, Spain, Australia, Syria, New Hebrides, Mesopotamia, Oregon. Sketched from First Drawings *by Sylvia Fein.*

Great people have been using drawing to make sense of ideas throughout history.

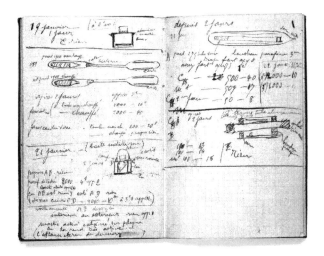

Marie Curie thought in words, numbers and scribbles.

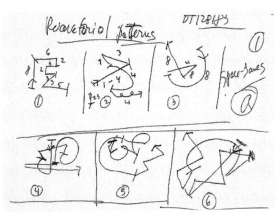

Merce Cunningham, famous choreographer, worked out his dances on paper.

REASON TO DRAW NO. 1: COMMUNICATION

Words are abstract. When I say "chair," what do you picture?

Maybe neither of these?

If I asked you to buy a chair, how would you know what to get? Better draw a picture!

Michelin three-star chef Michel Bras uses drawings to communicate to his pastry chef exactly how his cake should look (from *The Notebooks of Michel Bras: Desserts*). M. Bras mixes words and images to make sure his team understands what he wants, and thus he keeps his three-star rating.

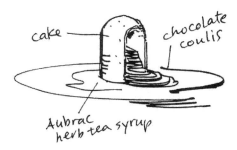

M. Bras sketch from The Notebooks of Michel Bras

Noelle Stransky, UX strategist, uses sketches to work through early ideas with her clients. Sketches invite non-drawers to join in, scribbling and annotating.

Taylor Reese, UX designer at Devfacto, draws pictures of key ideas during meetings. Draw what people say and everyone knows you're talking about the same thing.

REASON TO DRAW NO. 2: BETTER PROBLEM SOLVING

Have you ever been stuck when trying to figure out a problem?

It's hard to visualize all the details of a solution while simultaneously remembering all the parts of the issue.

But when you draw, you get things out of your head and into the world where you can see them. Hang your pictures on the wall to act as an external memory!

Throughout this book I'm going to have guest essays from people who using drawing in their work.

Here is the first one!

DAN BROWN ON DRAWING TO SOLVE PROBLEMS

Dan Brown is a founding partner in EightShapes, a Washington DC-based design consultancy. He is also the Author of Communicating Design, Designing Together and Practical Design Discovery.

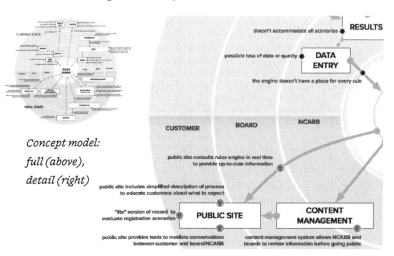

Concept model: full (above), detail (right)

"A client challenged me to model a concept central to their business. We sought to improve the technical infrastructure for this concept, which they called rules engine. The final model displayed three actors as circular "swim lanes," though perhaps "concentric wading pools" is better. The engine sat in the center of these, a hub through which information passed to each of these actors through different software components."

"I dug up my initial sketches, which reveal how I came to understand the domain as well as modeling it. Each iteration added something different."

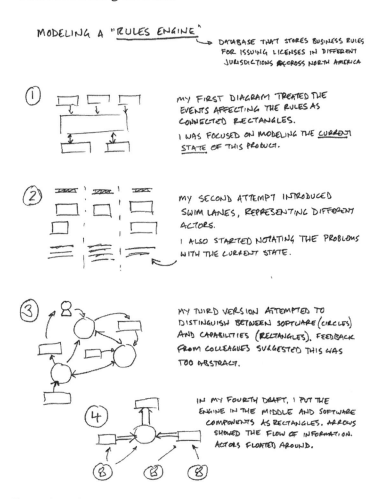

MODELING A "RULES ENGINE"
→ DATABASE THAT STORES BUSINESS RULES FOR ISSUING LICENSES IN DIFFERENT JURISDICTIONS ACROSS NORTH AMERICA

① MY FIRST DIAGRAM TREATED THE EVENTS AFFECTING THE RULES AS CONNECTED RECTANGLES.
I WAS FOCUSED ON MODELING THE CURRENT STATE OF THIS PRODUCT.

② MY SECOND ATTEMPT INTRODUCED SWIM LANES, REPRESENTING DIFFERENT ACTORS.
I ALSO STARTED NOTATING THE PROBLEMS WITH THE CURRENT STATE.

③ MY THIRD VERSION ATTEMPTED TO DISTINGUISH BETWEEN SOFTWARE (CIRCLES) AND CAPABILITIES (RECTANGLES). FEEDBACK FROM COLLEAGUES SUGGESTED THIS WAS TOO ABSTRACT.

④ IN MY FOURTH DRAFT, I PUT THE ENGINE IN THE MIDDLE AND SOFTWARE COMPONENTS AS RECTANGLES. ARROWS SHOWED THE FLOW OF INFORMATION. ACTORS FLOATED AROUND.

"Drawing pictures helps me get my head around a new idea."

REASON TO DRAW NO. 3: REMEMBER BETTER

I love listening to presentations, but I struggle with a couple of things:

1. ATTENTION: It's hard to focus! What's happening on Twitter? Is that a squirrel outside?

2. RETENTION: I get inspired by a TED talk one week and can't remember it the next one!

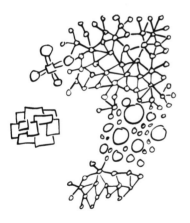

Doodling helps. People who doodle remember 29%[1] more information than those who don't.

Sometimes during a boring lecture I draw abstract forms just to quiet my mind. But if you want to get even better at listening, understanding and retaining information, try **sketchnoting**.

When you sketchnote, you draw pictures of the ideas you hear or read. More on page 79!

---

1. Andrade J. 2010 'What Does Doodling do?' *Applied Cognitive Psychology*

PART 1:

HOW
TO
DRAW

"A line is a dot that went for a walk."
—Paul Klee

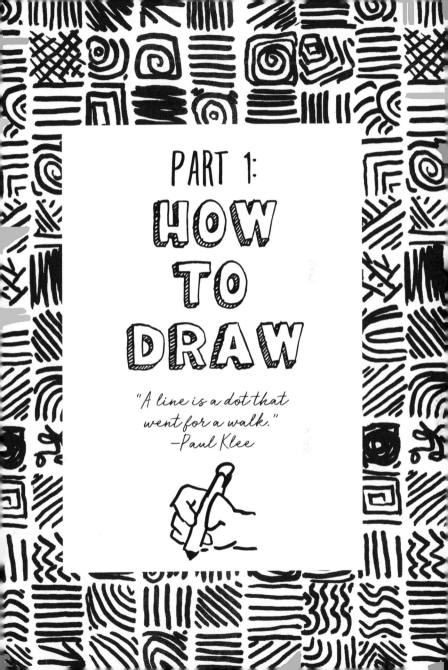

ARE YOU AFRAID TO DRAW?

"I CAN'T EVEN DRAW A STRAIGHT LINE"
SHE CRIED!

No one expects to sit down at a piano and play Chopin without practicing. So why do *you* expect to draw wonderfully without doing your scales?

Like any skill, from piano to basketball, you have to practice.

You will suck for a while.

But not forever.

START WITH LINES

If learning to draw is like learning to play piano, then **lines** are our scales.

Do them every day.

Begin by drawing lines in sets of five. Go in both directions, up and down.

Try to make the lines equidistant. Try to make diagonal lines, too.

Play with drawing the lines very close to each other, and very far apart.

Overlap your lines to make grids. If the lines are equidistant, you'll make tidy squares.

Try making lines very long.

when...

do you...

lose control?

Fill pages with lines during boring meetings.

EXERCISES

Listen to a song, and let your pen dance to it!

Fill grid paper with patterns of lines.

PRACTICE MAKING SHAPES

Start with **boxes**.

Let's think about how we make a box. Do you draw it all in one go, not lifting your pen up? Is your last line sloppy?

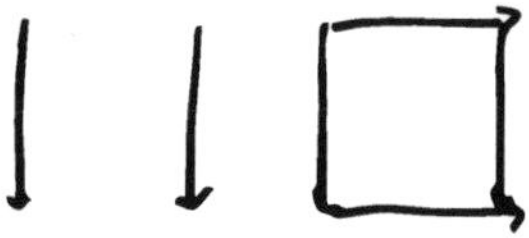

Play with different ways to draw them. Draw the vertical lines equidistant, then the horizontals.

Try drawing two L shapes. Does a certain technique make a better box?

Pull
Push

Left–Right   *Right–Left*

Are you more accurate when you **pull** or **push** the pen? Left to right? Right to left?

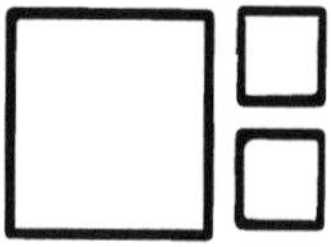

Try to make small boxes and big boxes, but always **stay square**!

From here, you can try making **rectangles**.

FREEHAND
VS.
RULER

JUST A SEC!

ZZZ

Next try **circles**. Circles are *really hard* to draw… if you rush.

Go slow!

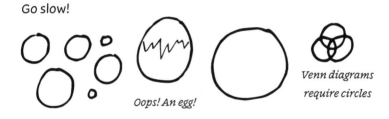

Oops! An egg!

Venn diagrams require circles

Keep circles tidy. Make sure the end point neatly touches the beginning point.

You don't want your circles embarrassed because the other kids at school say they are funny looking.

Finally, **triangles**. Making a triangle isn't as hard as it looks.

Draw a line. Mark the midpoint. Make a dot above the midpoint where you want your point. Now all you have to do is connect each end with the dot.

Practice your triangles. Make sure you close the corners!

Sierpinski triangle, fractal fans!

Arrows are just rectangles and triangles together.

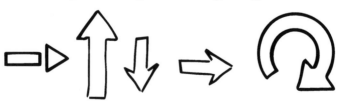

Or sometimes a triangle and a circle.

3-D SHAPES

Sometimes you need to make things 3-D. For example, if you wanted to draw a package.

For a **cube**, draw a square, then half a square behind it. Connect the corners.

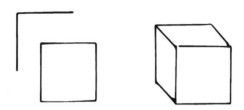

For a **pyramid**, the triangle's bottom line gets a point as well.

Spheres don't have hard edges to suggest 3-D surfaces. Give it a reflection, or consider shading.

SHADOW & TEXTURE

You can use lines to fill in shapes to create an illusion of shadow and depth.

Hatching

Crosshatching

Stippling

Scribbling

In **hatching,** lines go one way. In cross hatching, they are perpendicular. Stippling is made with dots. Scribbling is scribbling. But thoughtful scribbling!

You can make the texture shadowy two ways. Lines that are closer together look darker.

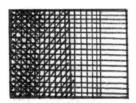

You can also crosshatch in different directions, building up density. Experiment!

EXERCISE

Fill a page with squares, rectangles, circles and triangles. Play with rulers and try freehand. Shade them. Fill with texture.

DRAW TO RELAX.

There is a kind of drawing meditation called **zentangles**. In this practice, you fill shapes with patterns.

This is a great way for you to practice your hand control.

And chill out.

Go back to your wandering lines (from page 29), and fill them in with patterns.

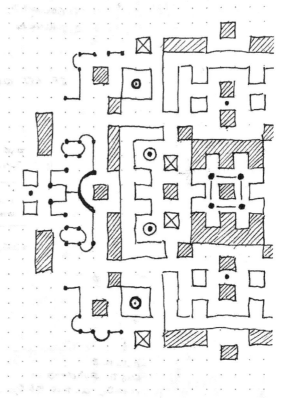

"I'm obsessed with the grid pattern on the paper. Practicing with grids sometimes results in interesting mechanical insights thrice removed."

—*Daniel Cook, Chief Creative Officer (and Game Designer) at Spry Fox*

HOW BAD IS YOUR HANDWRITING?

Is it worse than mine was in 2014?

I can barely read my own journal. But with practice, things can change for the better.

By 2016, you can finally read it.

It's been a long slow crawl to legibility. Practice!

A B C D E F G H I J K

Do you want to be understood?

L M N O P Q R S

The secret is to **slow down** and focus on the shape of the letters.

T U V W X Y Z

Practice lettering to relax and chill out, like you do with zentangles.

a b c d e f g h i j k

Focus on the **shape** of each letter.

l m n o p q r s

Make round letters **really** round. Make pointy letters **extra** pointy.

t u v w x y z

Feel each shape.

PERSONALIZE YOUR ALPHABET

Make the letters your own.

Kate Rutter, graphic facilitator extraordinaire, recommends starting with these variations.

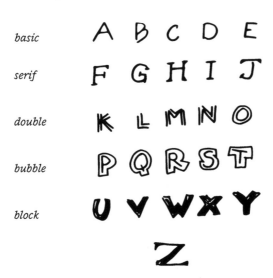

basic   A B C D E

serif   F G H I J

double   K L M N O

bubble   P Q R S T

block   U V W X Y

Z

They're great for making strong headers on whiteboards!

Find your own style of writing. There are a lot of ways to make an "a"

a, a, a, a, a, a a,

Try slanting letters, or replacing some with a shape.

OCGQAEFH \VO/\ΔN

Find famous architect's writing, and copy them!

PLAYHoUSE
OAKPARK

Copied from Frank Lloyd Wright...

ADDITIONS
NOTES

and from Bruce Goff

Try writing a favorite quote in your new style!

GIVE A\VAY LoVE LiKE
YoU'RE /\AD E oF IT.

– BRUCE GOFF

EXERCISE

Pick a font you like, and copy it by hand.

This is my take on Dave Pentland's "Steadman," a font based on the art of Ralph Steadman.

BECOME A FAN OF GOOD ENOUGH

We worry too much about drawing well. The human mind is great at seeing patterns everywhere.

We see faces in electrical sockets and cars (it's called pareidolia).

Most people can understand even the worst drawing.

If you try to be perfect, you may give up, when good-enough drawings do the job.

Try it yourself!

1. Draw a squiggle.

2. Make something!

EXERCISE

Make these squiggles into faces, people, creatures, or even birds!

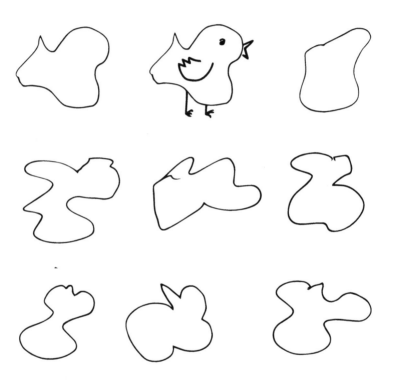

To become even better at drawing, use this human ability to see patterns and forms everywhere. In the next section, renowned visual thinker and graphic facilitator Kate Rutter will explain how. Learn more about Kate at http://intelleto.com

7 Ways of Seeing

Expand your visual skills by sketching something 7 different ways

When you draw an object, you understand it in a whole new way.

Use these **7 techniques** to...

→ Improve your observation skills

→ Sharpen your sketching skills

→ Expand your visual vocabulary with clear and accurate pictures of lots of objects.

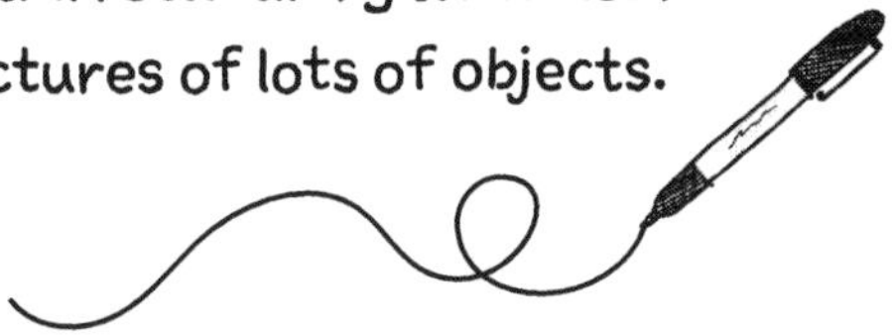

Before you begin:

Grab some paper and a pen. Sharpies are great... they smell like ideas. But they can bleed through your paper. Be advised. ;)

Choose something to sketch. You can pick something small (like a flower or a shoe) or something in the landscape (like a car or a tree.) You should be able to see it clearly, and have it not move for about 10 minutes.

Each of the 7 techniques has a suggested time limit, but if you need more (or less) time, that's a-okay.

When starting out, it's a good idea to pick something simple. As you get more practice, it's a lot of fun to sketch something complicated, or something that moves.

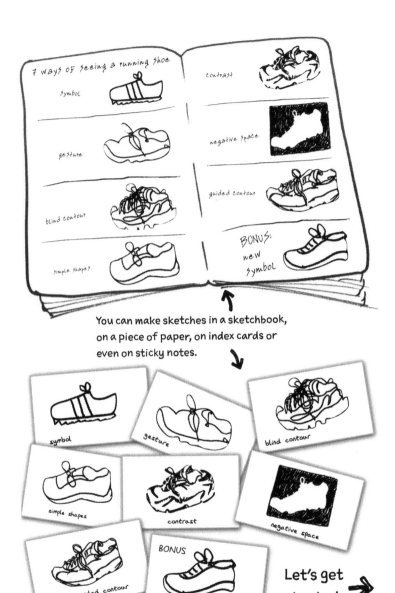

7 ways of seeing a running shoe

symbol

gesture

blind contour

simple shapes

contrast

negative space

guided contour

BONUS: new symbol

You can make sketches in a sketchbook, on a piece of paper, on index cards or even on sticky notes.

symbol

gesture

blind contour

simple shapes

contrast

negative space

guided contour

BONUS

new symbol

Let's get started →

1

Symbolic

🕑 10–15 seconds

Without looking at the object, draw a simple version of it. Sketch the "idea" of the object, not a picture of the specific thing.

tree! →

2

Gesture

🕑 3–5 seconds

Look at the object and make a **very quick** sketch of it, using only a few lines. Try to capture the "energy" and "movement" of the shapes. Work **super fast!**

3

Blind Contour

🕑 1-2 minutes

Without looking at your pen or paper, use your eyes to "trace" the edges of the object, while simultaneously using your pen to draw the outline in a steady, continuous line. Don't look at your paper! Go slow.

Tip: Your sketch probably won't look **anything** like the object. That's okay! But there will usually be parts that are awesomely accurate.

4

Simple Shapes

🕑 1-2 minutes

Stare at the object and break it down into basic shapes in your head. Aim for 3-4 shapes...no more than 6! Draw the shapes on your paper.

Tip: Think of a stained glass window.

5

Contrast

⏱ 2–3 minutes

Stare at the object and identify the shadows and darkest parts. Draw ONLY the darkest parts. Don't draw outlines or lines unless they are the darkest parts.

Tip: Squint your eyes to see the contrast more clearly.

6

Negative Space

⏱ 2–3 minutes

Draw the space AROUND the object. Try to get as much detail in the shape as possible. When you're done, draw a box around the shape and quickly fill it in.

7

Guided Contour

⏱ 3-4 minutes

Look intently at the object and use your eyes to "trace" the edges of the object, while simultaneously using your pen to draw the outlines and shapes. Glance back and forth between the object and your paper. Try to get as much accurate detail as possible while still working at a quick pace.

Tip: This is just like Blind Contour, but you get to look at your paper.

✳

BONUS!

New Symbol

⏱ 10 seconds

Using all your new knowledge, sketch an updated "symbolic" version. You'll find that your new symbol is **more accurate** than the previous one.

Try different layouts and ordering to see what works best for you.

symbol

gesture

blind contour

simple shape

contrast

negative space

guided contour

new symbol

A tree, 7 ways

#1

#2

#3

#4

#5

#6

#7

bonus!

Share your work on Twitter and Instagram tagged as #7WaysofSeeing

When you use the **7 Ways of Seeing** to explore the world, you'll begin to notice new things...more details, patterns in nature, and how things are put together. You'll also become faster and more precise with your sketching.

All these tricks help you build a rich, expressive and accurate visual vocabulary.

Have fun!

LET'S MAKE PEOPLE!

Since we are all people, and your coworkers are probably people, and your customers are people, let's learn to draw people.

Let's start with tiny people. Imagine they are far, far away. Here are some styles to try.

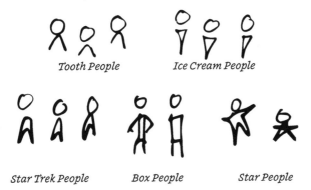

Tooth People *Ice Cream People*

Star Trek People *Box People* *Star People*

Try drawing a page full of tiny people. What feels good? What looks good?

You can give Star Trek people better proportions, and they look like architecture drawings.

You can add personality by giving clothing to your star people.

A BETTER STICK FIGURE

Most folks default to stick figures if they have to draw a person. They are easy but boring. We can do better.

Dan Roam, author of "Back of the Napkin," gives stick figures some personality by adding hands, feet and hair.

Dave Gray, founder of Xplane, starts with a parallelogram torso, then adds head and limbs.

Ivan Brunetti, New Yorker cartoonist, teaches his students to start with very simple geometric figures.

A circle, a triangle, and a few wavy lines and you can draw a person filled with existential angst.

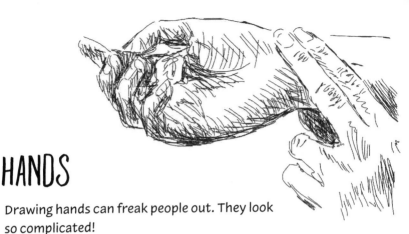

HANDS

Drawing hands can freak people out. They look so complicated!

But you don't have to draw them perfectly to get your ideas across.

A hand is just a circle with some digits hanging off of it. Keep your drawings simple. Cartoonists do this all the time. They draw hands with three fingers, or none!

This guy, drawn in the style of David Sibbet, only needs a finger to make a point. Simplifying the hand to a blob with one digit helps put focus on the gesture.

Mr. Trunk and Mr. Beak say:

THUMBS UP
TO THUMBS!

THUMBS
DOWN
TO FINGERS!

Drawn in the style of Lynda Barry. Read her books Picture This *and* What It Is *for drawing confidence*

You can either practice drawing hands until you master them, or stop worrying, and focus on just one finger.

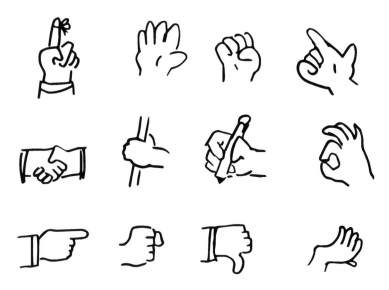

FACES

Because of pareidolia, it doesn't take much effort to make a face. Hugh Dubberly, information designer, makes faces with the letter "e."

Bill Verplank, interaction designer, uses lighting and a dot. He often adds a hand so his people can act on the world.

I draw quick faces like this. It's just a circle that ends a bit farther to the right, making a nose.

When I'm drawing on the whiteboard, I don't want to think about how to draw a person. I just focus on the ideas.

When people draw a smiley face, they often put the eyes too high. This makes the face look inhuman.

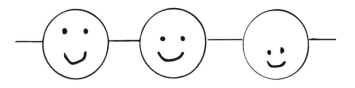

The eyes should be in the middle of the head.

If you put them lower, though, the face will look like a child's.

Here I am, to explain **face proportion**!

My eyes are in the middle of my face.

My nose is between my eyes and my chin.

My mouth is at the midpoint between the tip of my nose and my chin.

Our **bodies** have a **standard proportion** as well.

Humans are 7 "heads" tall.

Our legs take up half of our bodies.

Stand up and let your arms hang naturally. Your hands fall at your thighs.

The top part and bottom part of arms and legs are the same length.

It's not just me, all faces and body proportions are the same... if they are average.

But why be average?

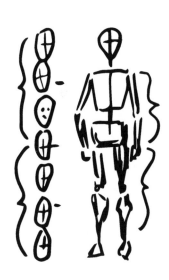

Heroic figures are drawn as being 8.5 heads high.

This Wonder Woman drawing I copied from a coloring book appears to get all her extra height from her legs.

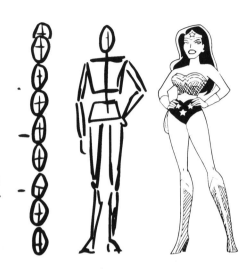

Children and cute cartoon characters (in manga, they are called "chibi") are 5 or 6 heads high.

Childish proportions places emphasis on the face, which shows emotion.

Play with proportion!

Wonder Woman © DC Comics, Inc

What does changing the **mouth** size do?

How about the **eyes**?

Eyes and mouths message **emotion**!

Try playing with the eyes, but leaving the rest of the face the same.

Now try combining mouth and eyes. How many emotions can you represent? How about other features?

Noses rarely show emotion, but they do give a hint about the character.

Top it all off with a hat or hairstyle!

Exercise: Eyebrows

This is an exercise from cartoonist Chris Ware. Fill a page with circle faces, and try just changing eyebrows. How many emotions can you create?

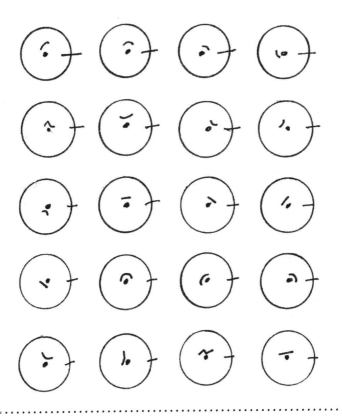

Next! Illustrator Eva-Lotta Lamm explains how to take your drawing to the next level! (see more at http://www.evalotta.net)

ON (FORMAL) CLARITY AND WALKING DOTS

by EVA-LOTTA LAMM

@evalottchen
www.sketchnotesbook.com
www.sketchinginter-faces.com

WHEN WE **COMMUNICATE**, WE WANT TO BE **CLEAR**.

THERE are **3 LAYERS** of **CLARITY** to MASTER:

CONCEPTUAL CLARITY

CONCEPT · STRUCTURE · FORM

- The CONCEPT is SOUND
- MAIN POINTS are SUMMARIZED well.
- GOOD EXAMPLES to ILLUSTRATE
- GOOD STORIES to add CONTEXT & COLOUR

STRUCTURAL CLARITY

- ELEMENTS are in a CLEAR ORDER
- ELEMENTS are LAYED OUT CLEARLY
- RELATIONSHIPS and HIERARCHIES are made VISIBLE.

FORMAL CLARITY

IN SKETCHING

- LINES are CLEAR & CONFIDENT
- Each element IS LEGIBLE
- INFORMATION-to-INK RATIO HIGH. Each line is there for a REASON
- VISUAL NOISE is REDUCED

IN SPEAKING

UMM...SO... what happened is... kind of like THIS...UMM, I think...

THIS is how I solved the PROBLEM

- VOICE is CLEAR & CONFIDENT
- CLEAR PRONUNCIATION & no MUMBLING
- WORDS are WELL CHOSEN, NO FILLER-WORDS.
- NO „UMMS" & „AHHS" DISTRACTING from the CONTENT

GOOD FORM is the FIRST THING that GOES when we are under **PRESSURE**.

FORM ↘

- ⏱ TIME PRESSURE
- 😰 BEING NERVOUS 😰
- 💰 HIGH STAKES
- 💡 LOTS of EXCITING IDEAS rushing in our HEAD.

PRESSURE →

HOW to **DEVELOP** GOOD FORM and **MAINTAIN** it under PRESSURE?

② OVER TIME, with FOCUSSED **PRACTICE**, WE BUILD **MUSCLE MEMORY** in our HAND.

① At FIRST, we need a lot of CONCENTRATION and **AWARENESS** to MAINTAIN FORMAL CLARITY.

④ The MUSCLE MEMORY **FREES UP CAPACITY** in the MIND to FOCUS on other THINGS.

③ THE well-PRACTICED HAND has **INTERNALIZED** the right WAY of MOVING to PRODUCE **CLEAR & CONFIDENT LINES.**

INTERNALIZATION		EXPERIENCE		PRACTICE		AWARENESS
	develops through		gained during		with	
sharper motor skills / muscle memory / CONFIDENCE		observing, perceiving, reflecting on IMPACT of my ACTION		REGULAR ACTIVITY / REPEATING over a LONGER PERIOD of TIME		FOCUS / OBSERVATION without JUDGEMENT

AS OUR **GOAL** IS TO DEVELOP a **CLEAR &
CONFIDENT LINE**, LET'S TALK ABOUT
LINES for a BIT...

" A LINE IS A DOT GOING for a WALK. "
↳ I LOVE this METAPHOR! —PAUL KLEE

WHEN WE **SKETCH**
WE SEND A DOT ON
A WALK.

the DOT CAN...

THERE are ONLY **4**
DIFFERENT **MOVES**
the DOT CAN PERFORM:

① GO **STRAIGHT**

MAKING a CONTINUOUS
STRAIGHT LINE.

② GRADUALLY CHANGE
DIRECTION, MAKING
a **CURVE**

the CURVE can range
from GENTLE to STEEP.

③ ABRUPTLY CHANGE
DIRECTION, making a
CORNER

The ANGLE of the CORNERS
can VARY, but the CHANGE
is always IMMEDIATE.

④ **JUMP**, LEAVING the
PAPER in ONE POINT &
LANDING in A DIFFERENT
PLACE.

this last MOVE
is not Really a
MARK-MAKING MOVE.
It is an OPPORTUNITY
to take a little BREAK,
OBSERVE and PLAN
the NEXT MOVE.

There can be TINY HOPS
or GIANT LEAPS across
the WHOLE PAGE.

With these **4 MOVES** we CAN **CREATE ANY SHAPE**. WE CAN **SKETCH ANYTHING** from a SIMPLE SQUARE to a complex OBJECT.

STRAIGHT & CORNER

CURVE & CORNER

STRAIGHT + CURVE + CORNER

+ JUMP:

OK... STRAIGHT, CORNER, STRAIGHT, CORNER, STRAIGHT, CUUURVE ...

+ SOME BASIC TIPS:

THE **KEY** to FORMAL CLARITY is to BE **CLEAR** ABOUT **WHICH** of the 4 **MOVES** YOUR DOT IS DOING at ANY POINT.

CORNERS are CORNES, NOT TINY CURVES.

THIS: ☐

NOT THIS: ▢

↳ IF you need, LIFT YOUR PEN after each STROKE to get clear CORNERS

LINES are NICE and CONTINUOUS. NO "FURRY" LINES!

THIS: ╱

NOT THIS: ～↑

take a DEEP BREATH, and then SLOWLY and CALMLY DRAW the LINE in an even PACE without STOPPING.

FIND the RIGHT SPEED:

IF your STRAIGHT LINES are BENDY, SLOW DOWN!

IF you have TROUBLE keeping your LONG LINES STRAIGHT, try drawing the LINES TOWARDS you.

IF your LINES are SHAKY, SPEED UP a BIT.

LET'S PRACTICE AWARENESS & FORMAL CLARITY...

LET'S GO!

① SEND a DOT for a WALK

→ TAKE an EMPTY SHEET of PAPER (LETTER / A4 or BIGGER)

→ PICK a STARTING POINT & LET your DOT EXPLORE the SPACE

→ The DOT can MOVE in any of the FIRST 3 WAYS explained earlier (LET'S LEAVE out JUMPING for NOW).

👁 BE AWARE of / OBSERVE:

↳ BEING CLEAR about WHICH MOVEMENT you are CURRENTLY PERFORMING. KEEP your AWARENESS with your DOT!

↳ what HAPPENS when you PLAY with different PARAMETERS... IN YOU → how does it feel? ON THE PAPER → how does the MARK change?

PLAY WITH:

→ SPEED of DRAWING

→ LENGth of TIME and DISTANCE between CHANGING MOVES

→ creating RHYTHM

→ which MOVES you CHANGE between

∞

→ Your BREATH. Are you HOLDING your BREATH? WHEN? DOES it CHANGE depending on the SPEED, RHYTHM or MOVEMENT?

JUST OBSERVE. DON'T JUDGE.

② GIVE your dot a COMPANION

↳ A FRIEND, walking ALONGSIDE your DOT at a RELAXED DISTANCE, CLOSE enough to HAVE a CHAT, but FAR enough to NOT BUMP into each other.

COMPANION Continued...

→ FOCUS on keeping the SAME DISTANCE throughout.

STAY AWARE about WHICH MOVEMENT you are DOING at any MOMENT.

FIND SOLUTIONS for CORNERS and TIGHT SPACES.

... maybe the COMPANION has to TRAVEL a LONGER DISTANCE or CHANGE DIRECTION in a different ANGLE or even a CURVE.

→ no MATTER which SOLUTION you CHOOSE, stay CLEAR about the MOVEMENT.

∞

Challenges:
→ KEEPING the exact SAME DISTANCE is HARDER

→ MORE SOLUTIONS for TURNS and CORNERS are NEEDED.

③ ADD a very CLOSE COMPANION

→ So CLOSE, they CAN WHISPER their MOST secret SECRETS to each OTHER.

Challenge: STAY SUPER CLOSE, but DON'T TOUCH!

∞

④ ADD a LOOSE COMPANION

THEY can SEE each ← other, but not REALLY TALK.
~ 3 TIMES the DISTANCE of original COMPANION.

BONUS: LET your DOT EXPLORE an OBJECT

→ PICK any RANDOM OBJECt on your DESK (or that you can SEE NEARBY).

→ LEt your DOT WALK along the EDGES of the OBJECT, EXPLORING its COMPLETE STRUCTURE.

→ when you REACH a DEAD END your DOT can JUMP.

AHA!

KEEP the same SHARP AWARENESS!

Copy,

In art school, we went to the museum to copy great artists.

Mod,

We learned to use the artist's approach to make derivative works.

ING YOU LIKE.

ReInvent,

As we worked, we began to mash up styles, find our own way of drawing.

Create

And then one day, we found our own voices, and we made something new. You can too.

WILLIE WONKA MEETS THE OMPA LOOMPA CHEIF

Chinese Emperor hats

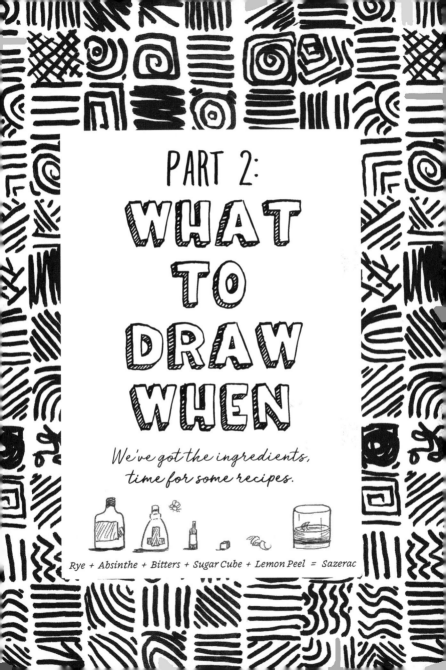

PART 2:
WHAT
TO
DRAW
WHEN

*We've got the ingredients,
time for some recipes.*

Rye + Absinthe + Bitters + Sugar Cube + Lemon Peel = Sazerac

HARD PROBLEMS TAKE A BETTER KIND OF THINKING

Scientists used to believe we used just our brain to think. But when problems get tricky, we use our brains *and our* bodies.

Who's never counted on their fingers and toes?

When problems are really tough, we need to get drawing. We draw to **see** what we **think**, in order to evaluate those ideas.

When ideas are made physical, they are tangible enough to understand and communicate. Scientists call this "distributed cognition." Business people call it "design thinking." Whatever you call it, it works!

In the second half of this book, you'll learn techniques used by a variety of professions to solve problems and invent new products. In each section, I'll show you real world examples as well as how to do the drawings yourself.

First, learn sketchnoting to **understand** and **remember** things we hear and read. Then learn to draw your customers, to better understand them.

Next, **draw to brainstorm**! We'll look at drawing for product design, and how we can use drawing to make sense of big data and complex ideas.

Finally, we'll **transform** our meetings with **pictures**.

Are you ready to turn your new skill into a **superpower**?

Sketchnotes by Jherin Miller from my Creative Founder class. Left is from Alex Osterwalder's talk on the Business Model Canvas, top is from Adam Nash's Five Sources of Traffic.

5 FORCES OF VIRAL TRAFFIC

① ORGANIC ② E MAIL ③ SEARCH ④ ADS/PARTNERSHIP ⑤ SOCIAL (FEEDS)

Google

MAKE SKETCHNOTES TO LISTEN AND REMEMBER

When I first started teaching at California College of the Arts, I was told the students wouldn't do the reading. And in the first class I taught, it proved to be true.

So when I taught a class again, I assigned the students to sketchnote all the reading.

Sketchnotes provided more than a way for me to check homework. Not only did they do the reading, they understood it more thoroughly and remembered it after.

What is sketchnoting? It's taking notes by drawing pictures of the ideas and words you hear. The Sketchnote Handbook, by Mike Rohde, had inspired an army of creative listeners to illustrate talks.

How do we do it? Let's ask Matthew Magain....

SKETCHNOTING

THE ART OF VISUAL NOTE-TAKING

© 2012 MATTHEW MAGAIN

SKETCHES HAVE BEEN USED FOR CENTURIES AS TOOLS FOR EXPLORING AND COMMUNICATING IDEAS...

THEY'RE USED IN HOLLYWOOD ...

... IN ARCHITECTURE ...

... AND IN DESIGN.

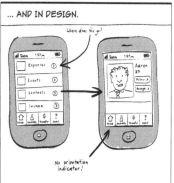

SKETCHING IS A FANTASTIC WAY TO EXPRESS YOURSELF — EVEN IF YOU'RE NOT AN ACCOMPLISHED ARTIST.

UNFORTUNATELY, SKETCHING IS FROWNED UPON BY SOME, MOST COMMONLY, WHEN IT OCCURS DURING CLASS.

PAY ATTENTION!

BECAUSE TAKING NOTES IS BEST DONE USING WORDS, RIGHT? **RIGHT?**

WHILE WRITTEN NOTES CAN FORM A GOOD **REFERENCE**, THEY'RE NOT NECESSARILY GREAT FOR **RECALL**.

PLUS THEY LOOK KIND OF BORING!

A GLOBAL MOVEMENT, KNOWN AS **SKETCHNOTING** (VISUAL NOTE-TAKING) IS GAINING POPULARITY, PARTICULARLY AT TECH CONFERENCES.

SKETCHNOTING USES A COMBINATION OF:

... WHICH MAKES IT SIMILAR TO THAT OTHER FROWNED-UPON ART FORM ...

COMICS!

LIKE THE ONE YOU'RE READING NOW!

A SKETCHNOTE DIFFERS FROM A COMIC IN AT LEAST TWO WAYS:

FIRSTLY, A SKETCHNOTE IS NOT STRICTLY **SEQUENTIAL** — THERE ARE NO PANELS TO INDICATE SEQUENCE. INSTEAD THE SKETCHER CAPTURES THE **ESSENCE** OF THE TALK AND ARRANGES IT AS SHE CHOOSES, IN A FORM OF **PERSONAL CURATION**.

SECONDLY, THERE ARE LESS BAD GUYS IN A SKETCHNOTE (UNLESS IT'S FROM A TALK ABOUT COMICS!)

GRRR!

© MARVEL COMICS

SKETCHNOTING REQUIRES YOU TO **MULTI-TASK**, WHICH MEANS YOU'RE OFTEN LISTENING, PROCESSING, AND DRAWING AT THE SAME TIME.

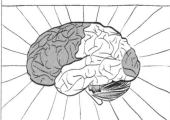

HOWEVER, YOU DON'T NEED TO BE AN ACCOMPLISHED ARTIST TO CREATE A GOOD SKETCHNOTE. SURE, IT HELPS, BUT REALLY YOU JUST NEED TO BE ABLE TO DRAW **BASIC SHAPES**.

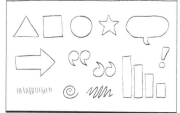

SO, WHY CREATE A SKETCHNOTE?

DOING SO FORCES YOU TO **PAY ATTENTION**. IT'S NOT MINDLESS DOODLING, IT'S CAPTURING INFORMATION CREATIVELY.

IT CAN IMPROVE YOUR **RETENTION** OF THE MATERIAL.

SKETCHNOTING CAN TURN AN OTHERWISE BORING PRESENTATION INTO A FUN **LEARNING** EXPERIENCE.

IN ADDITION, THE FINISHED SKETCH MAKES A USEFUL REFERENCE, A NOSTALGIC KEEPSAKE, OR EVEN A UNIQUE GIFT FOR THE PRESENTER.

SO, HOW DOES ONE GET STARTED?

THE NEXT TIME YOU'RE SITTING IN A TALK, START WRITING DOWN CONCEPTS THAT RESONATE WITH YOU. ARRANGE THE WORDS, ON THE FLY, IN AN INTERESTING WAY, WITH PERSONALITY.

Claire's holiday to **ITALY**

Flew to Rome, then caught the train to Venice.

5 hour trip

Travelled with her mum, dad and younger brother.

TRAVEL TIP:

" Are we there yet? "

Don't lose your passport !!

THROW IN A FEW QUOTES, AND MAYBE DRAW A SPEECH BUBBLE OR STYLIZED QUOTES AROUND THEM.

START EXPERIMENTING WITH DIFFERENT SHAPES THAT REINFORCE THE MESSAGE, AND WORK UP TO SKETCHING OBJECTS.

Travelled with her mum, dad and younger brother.

Flew to Rome, then caught the train to Venice.

DON'T WORRY ABOUT CAPTURING EVERYTHING — YOU'RE NOT CREATING A DEFINITIVE REFERENCE. AND REMEMBER, IT TAKES PRACTICE. OVER TIME YOUR SKETCHNOTES WILL IMPROVE, AND SO WILL YOUR LISTENING SKILLS.

FOR LOTS OF EXAMPLES, VISIT SKETCHNOTEARMY.COM OR BROWSE THE "SKETCHNOTES" TAG ON FLICKR.COM.

http://sketchnotearmy.com

SKETCHNOTE ARMY

IF YOU'RE FEELING CONFIDENT, WHY NOT SHARE YOUR SKETCHNOTES ONLINE? I'D LOVE TO SEE SOME OF YOUR CREATIONS!

CHECK OUT MATT'S SKETCHNOTES, HAND-DRAWN VIDEOS, AND MORE AT SKETCHVIDEOS.COM.AU

WHAT SHOULD YOU LEARN TO DRAW?

Sunni Brown, author of Doodle Revolution, recommends getting good at six types of sketchnote elements. Of course, your imagination is your only limit!

6 fundamentals of Visual Notetaking

(1.) Letters
abcd...

(2.) Bullets

(3.) Frames

(4.) Connectors

(5.) Shadows
5X 10

(6.) Peeps

sunnibrown.com

FANCY SKETCHNOTE ELEMENTS...

Connectors and dividers

You can sketchnote speeches, books, or even your ideas. Now let's look at some sketchnote **examples**!

ADM. WILLIAM MCRAVEN

UNIV. OF TEXAS AT AUSTIN
COMMENCEMENT SPEECH 2014

1. MAKE YOUR BED EVERY MORNING.

2. FIND SOMEONE TO HELP YOU PADDLE.

3. MEASURE A PERSON BY THE SIZE OF THEIR ♥ NOT THE SIZE OF THEIR FLIPPERS.

4. KEEP MOVING FORWARD KNOW THAT LIFE IS NOT FAIR.

5. YOU WILL LIKELY FAIL OFTEN. IT IS PART OF LIFE.

6. SLIDE THE OBSTACLE HEAD FIRST.

7. DON'T BACK DOWN FROM THE BULLIES.

8. STEP UP WHEN TIMES ARE TOUGHEST.

9. START SINGING WHEN YOU ARE UP TO YOUR NECK IN MUD.

10. NEVER, EVER GIVE UP!

DAVID CARR
NYT JOURNALIST
COMMENCEMENT SPEECH
U. OF CALIFORNIA, BERKELEY
2014   SCHOOL OF JOURNALISM

SHORT BITS OF ADVICE

BE PRESENT
"IF YOUR HEAD IS IN YOUR PHONE, THE SCENERY NEVER CHANGES.

DON'T WORRY ABOUT DOCUMENTING THE MOMENT. EXPERIENCE IT!

TAKE RESPONSIBILITY
WHEN YOU CAME UP SHORT, JUST SAY SO. DON'T MAKE EXCUSES.

BE HONEST
IT'S NOT A TACTIC. IT'S A WAY OF BEING.
When you develop a Reputation for telling the truth, people tend to listen to what you have to say.

We're ALL BROKEN ONE WAY OR ANOTHER. TO PRETEND OR EXPECT OTHERWISE IS STUPID.

DON'T BE AFRAID TO BE AMBITIOUS
ARTICULATE YOUR GOALS
- but -

DO A GOOD JOB OF WHAT'S IN FRONT OF YOU.
WORKING ON YOUR GRAND PLAN IS LIKE SHOVELLING SNOW THAT HASN'T FALLEN YET.

DON'T JUST DO WHAT YOU'RE GOOD AT
IF YOU STAY IN YOUR COMFORT ZONE, YOU'LL NEVER KNOW WHAT YOU'RE CAPABLE OF.

I have a half a million followers on Twitter but the person who needs to know what I am doing is me. I need to experience this moment as it unfolds.

LEARN TO EXPERIENCE FRUSTRATION
* TEACHABLE MOMENT.

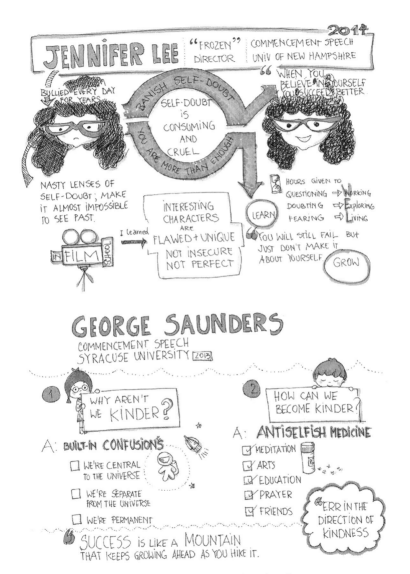

Sketchnotes from Cristina Negrut, creator & founder of
www.graduationwisdom.com

CHRISTINA WODTKE

don't change your OKR half way through
→ prepare to fail. OKRs are designed to push you a little more than you thought you were capable of

OKRs WORK IN A COMPANY
because they CASCADE

PRIORITIZE: conversations on what matters create ALIGNMENT!

ASK HARD QUESTIONS

COMPANY OKR

TEAM OKR — TEAM OKR

PROJECT TEAM OKR — PROJECT TEAM OKR

INDIVIDUAL OKR

↳ for personal growth and support of company goals
↳ Individual OKRs are about becoming better at your job.
↳ opportunity for manager-employee dialogue

OKRs ENABLE ALIGNMENT ACROSS TEAMS & PROJECT TEAMS. OKRs ENSURE THEY UNDERSTAND HOW THEY ARE CONTRIBUTING TO THE GREATER WHOLE. OKRs HELP COORDINATING WORK ACROSS TEAMS AND IN AVOIDING DUPLICATE WORK.

➡ DEPLOYING OKRs FOR A PRODUCT ORGANISATION FOCUS YOUR OKRs AT PRODUCT TEAM LEVEL. DISCUSS & PRIORITIZE LARGER OBJECTIVES AT LEADERSHIP TEAM LEVEL.

...JECTIVE (O):
...cuses a group or individual
...ound a **bold goal**
...alitative & Inspirational
- use language of / team
- must get you excited
...me Bound
...doable in 1month/1 quarter
...tionable by the team ...dependently
...ard but not impossible within ...imeframe by people/person ...at set it

OKR CONFIDENCE

OBJECTIVE: Establish clear value to distributers as a quality tea provider.

KR: Reorders at 85%	5/10
KR: 20% of reorders self-service	5/10
KR: Revenue of 250K	5/10

...EEK
...el with
...r flow
...les...

HEALTH

Team Health: YELLOW
team struggling with direction change

Distributer satisfaction Health GREEN

...OJECTS
...r notifications
...e flow for
...ributors on
...vice head.

KEY RESULTS (KR):
Quantify your objective by asking:
"How WOULD WE KNOW IF WE MET OUR OBJECTIVE?"

· Typically **3** KEY RESULTS
· Anything you can measure including:

Growth engagement Revenue Performance Quality

· Difficult, not impossible
"We really have to give all we've got, then maybe we'll make it!"

↳ SET **CONFIDENCE LEVELS**!

1/10 → never gonna happen
10/10 → easily nail this one
5/10 → 50% chance of failing

sweet spot, aim for this

...gs are for winners!
...ning high fail a lot.
...n't see how far you've ...gets depressing
...e tell about sales
...rescued customers,-
...CTS
...feel part of a special winning team
...s start looking forward to having something to ...e & speaks ...
...'company' starts to understand & appreciate what ...one does all day   Commit to WINNING

A sketchnote of a book I wrote, Radical Focus, drawn by Daryl Meier Fahrni

1 During **meetings**
Obviously that's the **NATURAL**
Way to **USE** Sketchnotes
Take **VISUAL** notes *and*
CATCH the *meaning*

2 explain **COMPLEX**
situations *and* visualize
BETTER the way to **SOLVE** it

3 Make Business
& IT understand
EACH OTHER by Improving
the **MEANING** of *Both Parts*

PROBLEM
Solving

BONUS
used for Business
specifications *and*
request analysis

Blue DRAFT

Advice from Marc Bourguignon http://sketchnotearmy.com /blog/2015/11/13/

sketchnoters-stories-sketchnoting-at-work-marc-bourguignon.html

DRAW YOUR CUSTOMERS

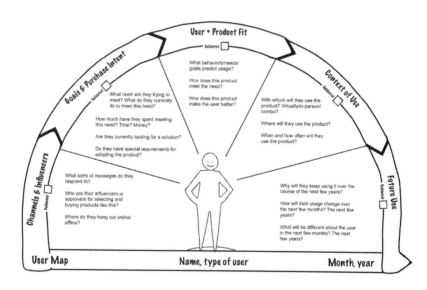

User Map from the book Build Better Products, *created by Laura Klein and illustrated by Kate Rutter because Laura does not draw if she doesn't have to.*

Even people who do not like to draw can use a customer canvas to visualize their customer's needs and wants and how those change over time.

Laura Klein is a product executive and bestselling author. She doesn't consider herself good at drawing, but she believes in its effectiveness. She partnered with Kate Rutter to create this canvas to make better product decisions. Simple drawings can create a powerful framework for understanding.

Sketch it on a whiteboard, and answer the questions on Post-its, then place them on the canvas.

Also, you can create empathy maps to understand customer psychographics and storyboards to understand customer behaviors.

EMPATHY MAPS

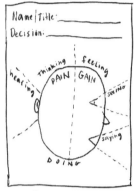

Empathy Map

Let's start simply. Let's make a picture of our customer point of view.

This tool is called the **Empathy Map**. It was invented by Dave Gray (his drawing on the left). You draw a quick sketch of your customer in the center, then use Post-its to develop a portrait of them in a moment in time.

Below is an empathy map created by my CCA students for customers of an audio management tool.

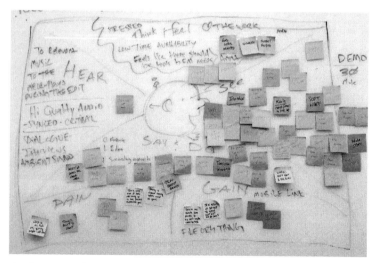

Student empathy map by Ridwan Pothigara, Tiffany Wang and Nathaniel Smith

THE CUSTOMER'S STORY

We can further understand customers by making **storyboards**. First, let me tell you about stories. All compelling stories share the same elements. Start with a character who wants something for a reason the audience can recognize. Harry Potter wants to defeat Voldemort to protect his new found home, Hogwarts.

The character struggles toward the goal, almost fails, but then succeeds through her own abilities, or with help. The story then resolves any open questions, and the character is changed.

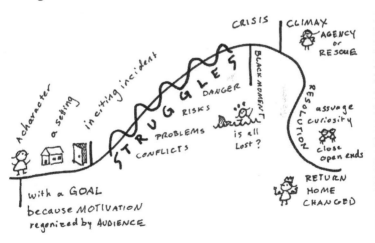

Our customers go through a similar journey...

CUSTOMER'S JOURNEY STORYBOARD

 To help your team at work understand how your product fits into your customer's lives, draw it out!

PANEL ONE: Show your key customer, their goal and motivation. What do they want? Why? Here we see a mom: "I want to lose weight to be healthy, so I can dance at my daughter's wedding someday."

PANEL TWO: The inciting incident. What makes the customer decide to journey toward her goal. "Oh my! I weigh what?!?"

PANEL THREE: How she currently tries to reach her goal, and how it fails her: "Exercise doesn't work!"

PANEL FOUR: Show what is at stake if she fails to reach her goal: "Oh no, high blood pressure!"

PANEL FIVE: Now your product or service can save the day.

"Diet bento boxes? Who knew!"

PANEL SIX: Show how the customer's life is improved.

Wei-Wei Hsu and Melissa Kim share storyboards for their new product.

Our Protagonist

Inciting Incident

Struggles

Crisis

Climax: Product as Hero

Changed Forever

DRAWINGS YOU NEED FOR STORYBOARDING

Communication Balloons: these symbols represent thinking, talks, whispering and shouting.

Emanata:

This is a term from cartoonist Mort Walker. It describes when the characters interior state manifests externally and visually.

Can you guess what's going on with these guys?

Layouts:

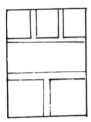

You could make a simple 6x6 by folding the paper in half, then in thirds. But what if you want to make one panel more prominent? Try different sizes and play with offsetting the panels to support your storytelling.

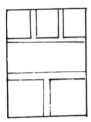 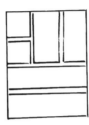 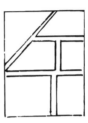 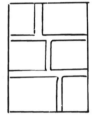

You may also need:

Objects from life, like a treadmill, or a doctor, or a scale giving up the ghost. Look for what makes the item recognizable.

Doctors have stethoscopes!

Collect drawings you make from life into an image library. Mike Rohde, author of *The Sketchnote Handbook*, tells you how!

Create a VISUAL Library

Build a library of icons you can use in your work and life, using squares, circles, triangles, lines, and dots.

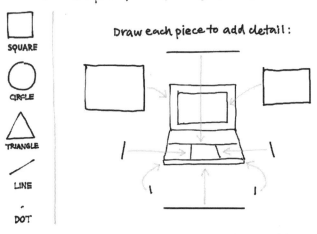

SQUARE

CIRCLE

TRIANGLE

LINE

DOT

Draw each piece to add detail:

Now, look around your space and draw what you see:

Phone

Tea

Logbook

Pen

You can also draw icons of concepts you use everyday:

Timesheet

Meeting

Project

Brainstorm

★ Keep your library icons <u>simple</u>! Try a variations. Steal ideas from The Noun Project!

Here are some ideas for creating your visual library:

CREATE PORTABLE VISUAL LIBRARY SHEETS

Tuck them into the back of your notebook.

Move them from notebook to notebook as you fill them up.

TITLE and notes about the sheet

write the library icon name, then draw your concept above.

use both sides

Or draw icons in the back of your sketchbook

HOW MANY ICONS can you create in 5 min?

Challenge your FRIENDS!

TAKE PHOTOS of your library entries with a smartphone and store them in a note-taking app for easy, searchable access (and as a backup).

★ Always carry a blank card so you're ready when boredom strikes!

Mike Rohde @rohdesign · rohdesign.com · sketchnotearmy.com

DRAW CONCEPT SKETCHES AND DIAGRAMS FOR BETTER BRAINSTORMS

DRAW YOUR IDEAS!

People who invent new things use drawings to explore ideas quickly, from cutting edge chefs to architects.

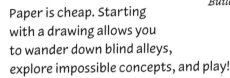

Building idea from Zaha Hadid, architect

Paper is cheap. Starting with a drawing allows you to wander down blind alleys, explore impossible concepts, and play!

There are two particularly useful types of drawings you use to brainstorm: concept sketches and concept models.

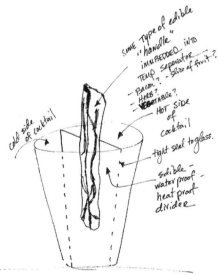

Sketch for a new cocktail by Grant Achatz of Alinea

CONCEPT SKETCHES

If you want to make something really innovative, you need to explore a lot of different ideas. Designer Damien Newman describes the creative process with this diagram. If I can paraphrase: You start a new project wandering around a bit, trying new things. Then you can pick the right idea to refine.

Drawing makes ideas tangible, so you can evaluate them. Then go go go!

Brian Gulassa is an award winning toy designer. He begins designing a new toy by creating dozens of Post-its holding tiny ideas represented with words and pictures.

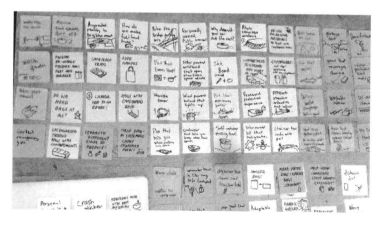

He then fleshes out the ideas that show promise on index cards.

Index cards have a nice surface for drawing, yet the small size keeps him from getting too caught up in details too early. Small paper keeps you working big picture.

Eventually Brian creates detailed sketches to explore the most interesting ideas and to share with his clients.

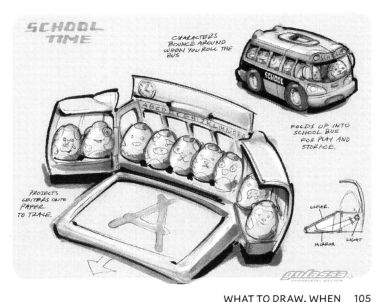

MAP ALL THE CONCEPTS!

When you start a new project, it's important to get your ideas out of your head and on to paper where you can see them.

MindMaps are a good place to start. They are like brainstorming on paper, free form and fast.

Start with an important idea. Free-associate more ideas, and connect them with lines.

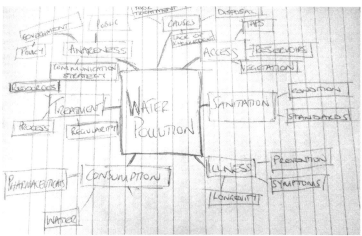

A MindMap for a game about water pollution by Andrew Reid

Rolf Faste, 1993. Courtesy of the Rolf A. Faste Foundation for Design Creativity.

MODEL YOUR IDEAS

A concept model helps us understand a complex system via pictures. We make concept models for ourselves, as we try to understand something. We make them for others to give them a framework for understanding what we've figured out. Concept models are not a complete map of a system, but rather an edited selection that tells a story.

They typically take one of three forms:

1. Elements

This model shows the elements of a system and the elements' relationships to each other. You might draw a game or a website or a business model—anything complicated is more easily understood with a model.

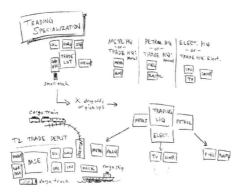

The elements can be layered, or parts of a whole, or overlapping. Vary the size of each element to express importance.

Stone Librande design, for SimCity

Even storytellers use concept models! A million drama teachers have drawn Freytag's triangle to explain the three act structure.

2. Processes

How do the elements change over time? Draw this, and you're drawing a process concept model. Game designers draw the core play loop, and process innovators draw a better way to work. The Lean Startup model (right) shows how companies can get smarter over time.

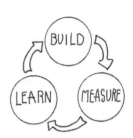

3. Comparisons

How does the screen look before and after the customer has logged in? What is the difference between us and our competitors? What do different kinds of customers prefer?

The 2x2 is a common comparison format. It can be drawn different ways, but it always represents opposing concepts, and where elements exist along a continuum.

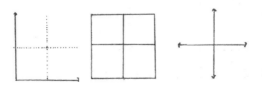

Here is Bartle's taxonomy of players. Richard Bartle researched online roleplaying games, and discovered that people played for different reasons. Some were competitive, some were social, and others just wanted

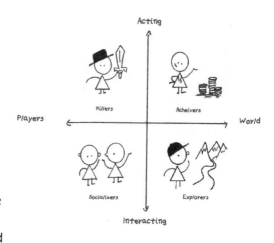

to explore. He wrote up a long research report, but it's his diagram that led his ideas to be widely adopted even beyond game design.

Bill Verplank's Model of Interaction Design

We make concept models for customers to explain our value. We make them for peers to share a new ideas.

We make concept models for teammates, when we want everyone to be on the same page.

And we make models when we are brainstorming new ideas, games, products and services!

EXAMPLES FROM GAME DESIGN

Game designs often create complex systems and economies. Think of SimCity or Civilization.

Game designers draw concept models and concept sketches to design how the game works, and then to communicate that vision to their team.

Here is a selection of examples from the sketchbooks of game designers. We can learn a lot from how they work.

Daniel Cook's Concept Sketches for SteamBirds.

STONE LIBRANDE

Lead designer at Riot Games. Games include SimCity, Spore, Diablo III and more!

Early brainstorming to explore the resource flows in SimCity.

I'm a visual thinker. In order to solve complex problems I need to see a picture of the solution. Although I have plenty of software tools at my disposal to accomplish this, the majority of my early design work begins in a small sketchbook that I carry with me.

A mechanical pencil is clipped to the inside of the spiral so that I always have a sharp point and eraser at the ready.

The sketching process is incredibly fast. When I am in "sketchbook mode," I am only concerned with explaining things to myself. Knowing that the sketches aren't meant for anyone else is liberating and absolves me from my perfectionist tendencies.

I scribble, cross-out, refine, erase and move onto a clean page when I can no longer decipher my own scrawls. When I get to the point where the vision is clear to me then I'll translate

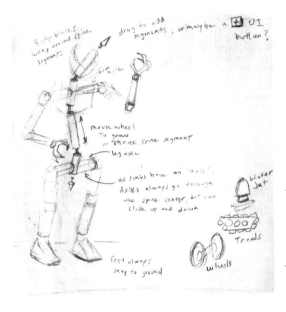

From sketch to deliverable for an unpublished expansion pack for the game Spore

Handwritten sketch notes:

Body blocks wrap around spine segments

drag to add segments, or maybe a ⊞ UI button?

mouse wheel to grow or shrink spine segment

leg axle

all limbs have an "axle". Axles always go through the spine center, but can slide up and down

Hover Jet

Treads

Wheels

feet always snap to ground

Robot Editing

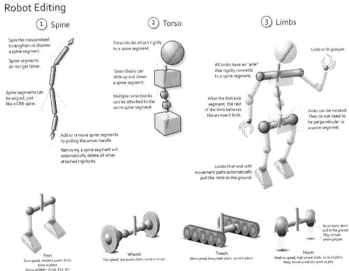

① Spine

Spin the mousewheel to lenghten or shorten a spine segment.

Spine segments do not get fatter.

Spine segments can be angled, just like a CRE spine.

Add or remove spine segments by pulling the arrow handle

Removing a spine segment will automatically delete all other attached rigblocks.

② Torso

Torso blocks attach rigidly to a spine segment.

Torso blocks can slide up and down a spine segment.

Multiple torso blocks can be attached to the same spine segment.

③ Limbs

Limb with grasper.

All limbs have an "axle" that rigidly connects to a spine segment.

After the first axle segment, the rest of the limb behaves like an insect limb.

Axles can be rotated. They do not need to be perpendicular to a spine segment.

Limbs that end with movement parts automatically pull the limb to the ground.

Feet
Slow speed, medium power drain, turns in place.
Bonus abilities: jump, kick, etc.

Wheels
Fast speed, low power drain, turns in one arc.

Treads
Slow speed, high power drain, turns in place.

Hover
Medium speed, high power drain, turns in place.
Note: Hover is not the same as jets.

Hover sorts don't pull to the ground. They remain where placed.

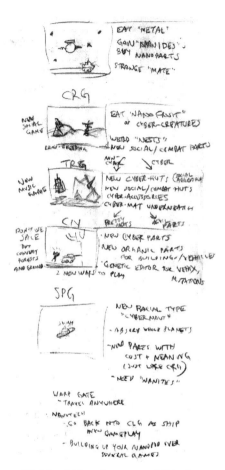

everything over to Adobe Illustrator and clean things up to make it understandable for others.

This technique works great on whiteboards, too. While not as private as a sketchbook, it is a great way for the team to brainstorm and contribute to the early design process. Everyone is given a marker and allowed to draw and erase interactively.

When we are all in agreement about the basic structure of the task then I copy it into a formal design document.

On a smaller team I've found that I can skip the clean-up step and let the "document" live on

High level ideas for an unpublished Spore expansion pack.

the whiteboard. When we are ready to move onto the next task, we take a photograph of the whiteboard for the archive, erase everything, and start on the next project with a clean slate.

DANIEL COOK

Chief Creative Officer of Spry Fox.
Games include Triple Town and Alphabear.

I'm usually working on multiple projects at once. As well as brainstorming future projects. I tend to mix drawings freely, jumping from one topic to the next depending on who I'm talking to or what task comes up. A lot like a white board really. The paper is just there as an external cache to facilitate distributed cognition.

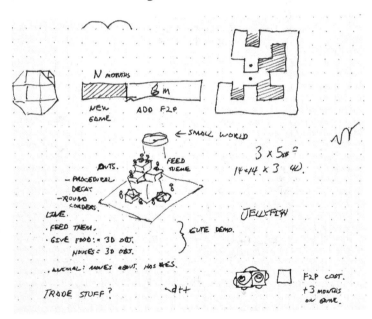

Brainstorming a game. This has a mix of scheduling details, thumbnail of what the game might look like and mechanical concepts or key questions that determine the constraints.

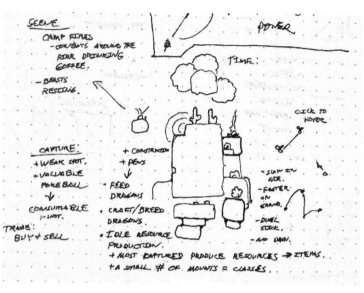

SCENE
- CAMP FIRES
  - COWBOYS AROUND THE FIRE DRINKING COFFEE.
- BEASTS RESTING.

POWER
TIME:

CLICK TO HOVER

CAPTURE:
+ WEAK SPOT.
+ VALUABLE POKE BALL
↓
CONSUMABLE 1-INST.

TRADE:
BUY + SELL

+ CONSTRUCTION
+ PENS
• FEED DRAGONS
• CRAFT/BREED DRAGONS.
• IDLE RESOURCE PRODUCTION.
+ MOST CAPTURED PRODUCE RESOURCES → ITEMS.
+ A SMALL # OF MOUNTS = CLASSES.

- SLOW IN AIR.
- FASTER ON GROUND.
- DUAL STICK.
- NO DMN.

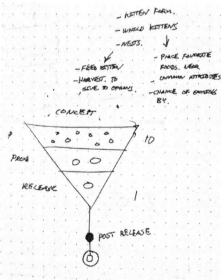

- KITTEN FORM.
- UNMELD KITTENS
- NESTS.
↓
- PLACE FAVORITE FOODS. NEAR COMMON ATTRIBUTES
- CHANCE OF GETTING BY.

- FEED KITTEN
- HARVEST. TO GIVE TO ORPHANS.

CONCEPT
10
PROD
RELEASE
POST RELEASE

Above: Another prototype concept. Very early stage. Includes both mechanics and world building. Scene: Campfire. Cowboys around the fire drinking coffee. Beasts resting.

Left: A kitten farming game.

ROBIN HUNICKE

Founder of Funomena, professor at UC Santa Cruz. Designer of Journey, Flower and Flow

I like to draw because it helps me clarify the shape of things. Specifically—I like to work out the symbols, patterns and forms that will recur throughout the experience.

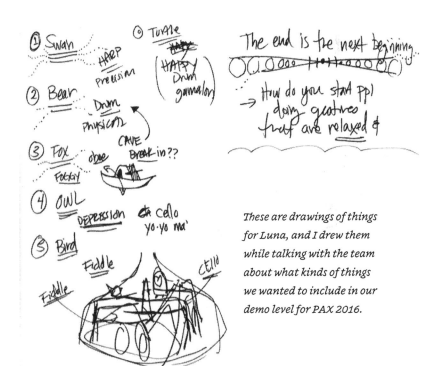

These are drawings of things for Luna, and I drew them while talking with the team about what kinds of things we wanted to include in our demo level for PAX 2016.

I also want to think about layouts, level designs, ways in which the player will perceive change as they move through the world. Sketching/storyboarding out moments that are in my head also helps me collect feedback and brainstorm with the artists, designers and engineers on a project.

This process continues throughout the game's development. In fact, I would say that during a typical meeting, I will draw at least once or twice in my notebook, on a whiteboard or sticky-note just to promote clarity and help solidify the ideas as they coalesce. Often, drawings are better than words

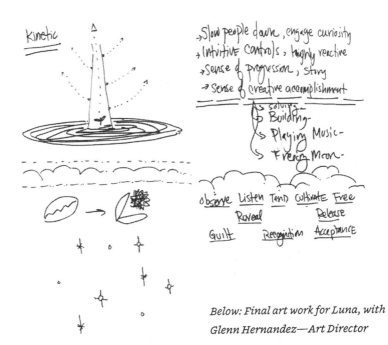

Kinetic

→ Slow people down, engage curiosity
→ Intuitive controls, highly reactive
→ Sense of progression, story
→ Sense of creative accomplishment
    ⤷ Solving
    ⤷ Building
    ⤷ Playing Music
    ⤷ Freeing Moon

Observe Listen Tend Cultivate Free
         Reveal   Release
Guilt   Recognition   Acceptance

Below: Final art work for Luna, with
Glenn Hernandez—Art Director

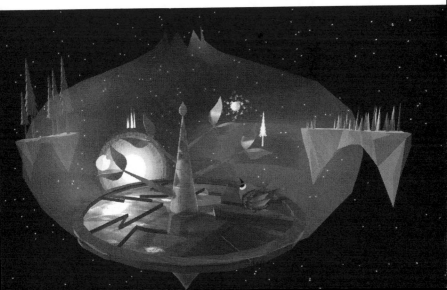

DRAW WHEN YOU ARE CREATING NEW PRODUCTS AND SERVICES

There are two types of sketch scenarios for me:

1. I'm talking through a problem with someone who is helping me figure it out. We're riffing together and I'm working very quickly, so those sketches are ultra messy. Some of my sketches are also quick re-creations of what's happening on a whiteboard.

2. I'm completely stuck on a problem with no idea how to proceed. Chatting with colleagues has not led to any particular insights, so I'm alone with my head down throwing out lots of paper. These sketches are just as messy, but usually contain a bit more detail.

— Alicia Loring, User Experience Designer

THREE USEFUL DIAGRAMS FOR DIGITAL PRODUCT DESIGN

If you work with a multidisciplinary team, you need a way to communicate clearly about the decisions you are making about your product.

Let's pretend we're making a cooking application!

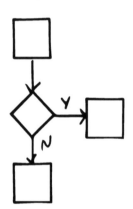

1. Flowcharts & Relationship Diagrams

The flowchart (or "flow" for short) is for user tasks. It's how you draw interaction. Is the user logged in? If not, show the log in screen.

The relationship diagram shows how the content is organized. Is tomato categorized as a fruit or vegetable?

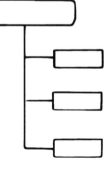

For example, you use the hierarchy diagram to show what categories are available when people are browsing recipes. You'd use a flow to show how the customer saves that recipe.

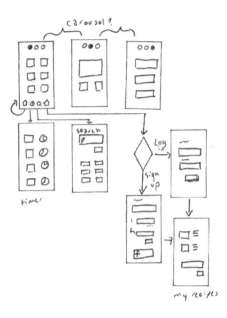

2. Wireflows

Add a little details to those flows and you've got wireflows.

These are useful to draw on a white board when collaborating with your team.

Use just enough details so your team knows what screens you are discussing.

3. Wireframes

You make these when you are figuring out the layout of your interface. There are a more detailed version of a wire flow screen.

Don't worry about being perfect. You're just thinking with a pencil. When you start getting fussy, it's time to add color, type and finalize the look and feel.

So what goes in those wireframes?

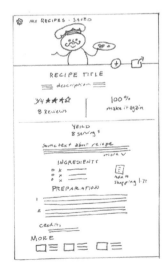

DRAWING INTERFACES

There are some shortcuts that designers use when sketching interfaces!

A box with an "X" means it's a picture. 3-D boxes are buttons. Parallel lines are the symbol for text blocks. A zigzag at the bottom means more beneath (for scrolling!)

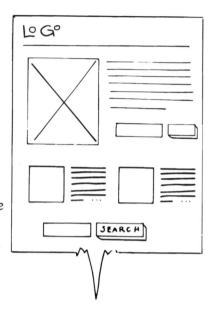

Draw dropdowns or radio buttons for mutually exclusive choices, or check boxes for when you can pick more than one item in the list... you can even show what's in your dropdown.

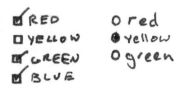

DRAWING DEVICES

You'll want to be able to draw devices when you are storyboarding your product.

Don't worry, the new devices are much easier to draw than the old ones were. For example, they have fewer buttons. Smart phones are just rectangles within rectangles.

A laptop is easier to draw than a desktop!

Exercise

Pick a website you visit every day, and sketch a wireframe.

ERIN MALONE

Erin Malone is a partner at Tangible UX, a professor at California College of the Arts, and author of Designing Social Experiences.

I draw to quickly capture ideas about interaction and language, and to explore the story of a person working through a system or application. When I am alone, I draw on paper—lately using 5x8 index cards or post it notes— that I can gather together and reshape and reorder."

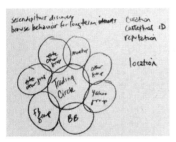
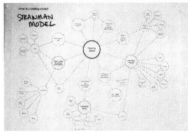

When I am working with clients, I draw on large post-it white paper or on white boards. Post-it paper lets me ideate around a topic or theme and gives me enough space for flows but are still movable and can be saved.

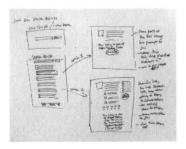

In team meetings, I draw on the white board to visually express the ideas we are exploring. This helps validate the shared understanding or lets us see if we are on wrong track.

Drawing helps clarify and crystallize an idea that the other person may have problems explaining. Sometimes I draw in tandem with someone else, sketching, erasing, oversketching/ overlapping, as we get into a flow of ideas. That

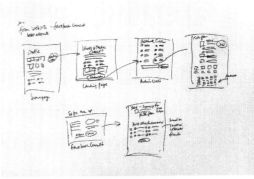

process is very empowering. What we co-create is stronger than work either would have created alone.

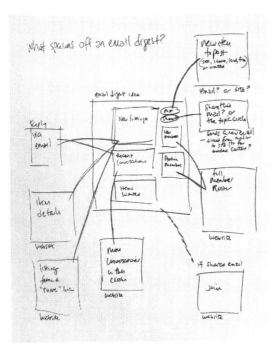

The images are from a project looking at how to encourage social engagement around selling items and using referral emails and email digests to show a community around a topic.

ALICIA LORING

Alice Loring is a User Experience Designer with 10 years experience in front-end mobile & web. She currently works at Riot Games.

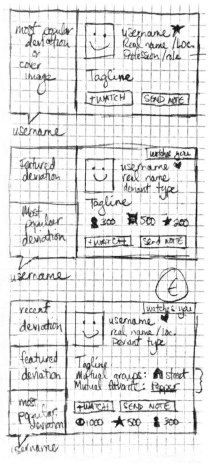

I've worked with designers I regarded highly, who seemed to crank out impossible work overnight. Even with the 8 years of experience I had at that point, it was a total mystery to me how they did it. They'd show up at the 10AM meeting with brand new, camera-ready work— as though they were geniuses who saw things in their mind's eye and made it exist simply by snapping their fingers.

Meanwhile, I sat at my desk struggling with design like a Rubix cube—no idea what the answer was, getting it wrong over and over.

Eventually I got a peek behind the curtain, and their process was more or less as imperfect and organic as my own. In fact, one of them told me I'd become a better designer by allowing my process to be even more messy, more unrefined.

Sometimes designers face a degree of social pressure to appear as though they have all the answers, and to let design resemble an ineffable black box to others. By sharing my sketches, I hope to upend that notion, and show that the early creative process is not glamorous; it's jumbled and uncertain; it's getting things wrong over and over... and maybe the occasional thing right.

All drawings: Ideation work for DeviantArt.com and DreamUp.

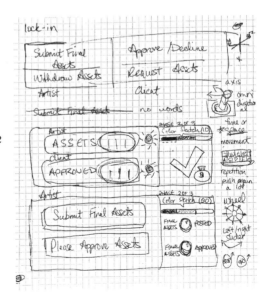

MAKE COMPLEX IDEAS AND DATA MAKE SENSE!

Proving your point with hard data is powerful, but lists of numbers are dull and confusing. Drawings are more compelling and easier to understand.

You might think scientists take thousands of points of data and pour them into an algorithm and magically out comes a chart, but you'd be wrong. It takes a human hand to explore potential metaphors and make raw data into a story.

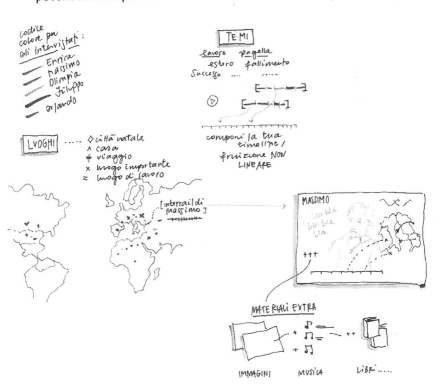

Visualization Sketches by Giorgia Lupi for the magazine Peninsula Hotel.

In *Good Charts*, Scott Berinato says there are four types of charts. You are either thinking, or you are communicating. You are either working with ideas, or with data.

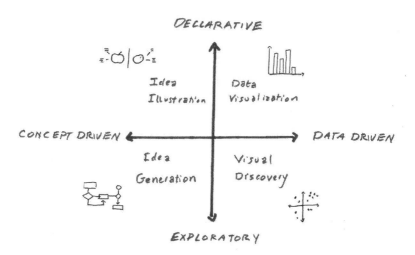

We looked at drawing for thinking when we made concept models for brainstorming.

Now let's look at charts that communicate. Stephen P. Anderson will start us off with the basics of designing infographics.

Stephen P. Anderson is a renowned visual thinker. He is widely admired for his information design skills, on display in his book, Seductive Interaction Design.

We use all kinds of

VISUAL MODELS to...

1. HOLD INFORMATION

2. REVEAL PATTERNS

AND YES...
3. TO COMMUNICATE!

"CHARTS"

"DATA VISUALIZATIONS"

"DIAGRAMS & DECISION MAKING MODELS"

"CANVASES, FRAMEWORKS, PLANNING TOOLS..."

... AND MANY MORE!

Even simple games like 'Tic Tac Toe' are models that hold information (X's & O's) and reveal patterns

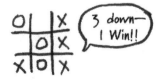

While these visual models are quite different from each other, they all share a common set of visual elements.

Let's use our tic-tac-toe example...

OBJECTS

EACH OF THESE MARKS IS AN OBJECT IN AN IMAGINARY GAME SPACE. AN 'X' OR AN 'O' INDICATES WHICH PLAYER MADE THAT MARK

PLACEMENT

THESE OBJECTS ARE ARRANGED RELATIVE TO EACH OTHER IN A WAY THAT HAS MEANING IN THIS GAME (3 IN A ROW IN ANY DIRECTION WINS!)

TERRITORY

TO CLARIFY THIS PLACEMENT WITHIN THE GAME SPACE, WE ADD CLEAR BOUNDARIES

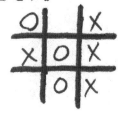

These exact same visual elements are present in how societies and nations have formed throughout history:

PEOPLE (OBJECTS) GATHERED OR GREW INTO FAMILIES AND TRIBAL GROUPS (PLACEMENT) WHO LATER DEFINED NATURAL OR AGREED UPON BOUNDARIES (TERRITORY)

Keeping with "people" as our OBJECTS, there are many other ways to think about PLACEMENT. We can organize people based on something...

LITERAL:

PEOPLE ON A CONTINUUM SORTED BY HEIGHT

CONCEPTUAL:

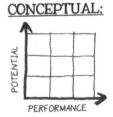

THE '9 BOXES MODEL' USED TO ASSESS EMPLOYEES

In all cases, the elements are the same: OBJECTS, PLACEMENT, TERRITORY

These exact same visual elements are present in how we manage projects:

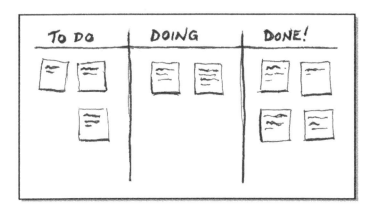

We have OBJECTS

 ← (STICKY NOTES)

We use PLACEMENT to cluster tasks:

 TASKS ARE GROUPED BASED ON COMPLETION STATUS

...and we define TERRITORY by the addition of lines and labels:

Even with something more complex, you find the exact same visual elements:

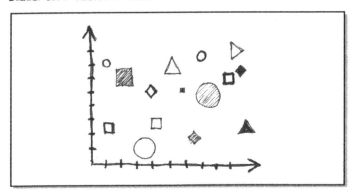

We have OBJECTS:

We use PLACEMENT to indicate specific & meaningful <u>points</u> (vs an area):

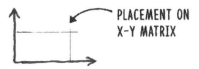

PLACEMENT ON
X-Y MATRIX

...and TERRITORY is defined by a very precise scale:

NOTE: WE COULD ALSO DEFINE
TERRITORY WITH REGIONS:

Let's examine each of these visual elements in more detail...

OBJECTS

Did you notice how OBJECTS have unique visual properties that differentiate them?

SHAPE

SIZE

ROTATION

PATTERNS

COLOR

MOTION

OUTLINE / NO OUTLINE

ETC.

Consider some of the visual properties available to us with our sticky note project board example:

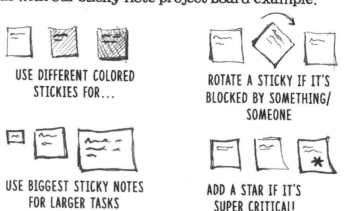

USE DIFFERENT COLORED STICKIES FOR...

ROTATE A STICKY IF IT'S BLOCKED BY SOMETHING/ SOMEONE

USE BIGGEST STICKY NOTES FOR LARGER TASKS

ADD A STAR IF IT'S SUPER CRITICAL!

These are all examples of using "visual encodings" to convey meaning!

There are dozens of visual encodings to choose from. But, it's critical to understand the FUNCTION of each:

TO SHOW PRECISE QUANTITY:

IT'S EASY TO SPOT SUBTLE DIFFERENCES IN <u>LINE LENGTH</u>

TO SHOW GENERAL QUALITATIVE INFORMATION:

<u>LINE THICKNESS</u> INDICATES RELATIVE STRENGTH OF CONNECTION

TO SHOW SEQUENCE

<u>COLOR + ROTATION</u> LETS ME KNOW IF I SHOULD BUY OR NOT...

TO SHOW CATEGORY:

<u>ICONOGRAPHY</u> DIRECTS ME TO THE RIGHT BATHROOM

Not all visual encodings function in the same way!

✳ NOT SURE WHICH VISUAL ENCODING TO USE? DOWNLOAD A HANDY-DANDY CHEATSHEET AT: <u>WWW.POETPAINTER.COM/VISUAL-ENCODINGS.PDF</u>

PLACEMENT

When we Arrange and/or Sequence things, we're using <u>spatial positioning</u> to convey meaning.

We already do this in many different ways. Consider how most of us sort dirty laundry:

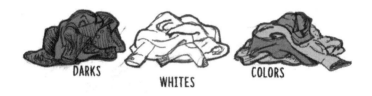

DARKS   WHITES   COLORS

...or how we arrange ingredients for use in a complex recipe:

"Hmm. Have I added the cinnamon yet, or not?"

Before the page, there was space itself. Perhaps the simplest way to use space to communicate is to arrange or rearrange things in it."

—Barbara Tversky

We can ARRANGE things...

INTO GROUPS

(THIS IS KNOWN AS
<u>CATEGORICAL</u>
ARRANGEMENT)

ALONG A PATH

WE USE <u>ORDINAL</u> ARRANGEMENT TO SEQUENCE THINGS

...AND IF THAT SEQUENCE USES A SCALE, WE
CALL THAT <u>INTERVAL</u> (OR <u>RATIO</u>) ARRANGEMENT

And the way we <u>SEQUENCE</u> things means something:

IN <u>VERTICAL</u>
SEQUENCES,
TALLER = MORE
OR BETTER

WITH <u>CENTRAL-</u>
<u>PERIPHERAL</u> SEQUENCING

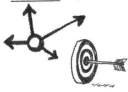

STUFF IN THE CENTER
IS MOST IMPORTANT...

WE TEND TO USE <u>HORIZONTAL</u>
SEQUENCE FOR TIME*

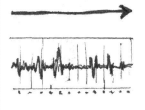

* IN WESTERN CULTURES

WE USE <u>RADIAL</u> SEQUENCING
FOR REPETITIVE CYCLES

...AND WE
USE <u>SPIRAL</u>
SEQUENCING
IF THERE'S A SMALL
CHANGE WITH EACH CYCLE

TERRITORY

Finally, it's generally good to make 'place' explicit for others. (remember our tic-tac-to board before we added lines?!). Here are some ways to define place...

ADD BOUNDARIES

HARD BOUNDARY

FUZZY BOUNDARIES

USE SHAPES

THINK ABOUT WHAT IS SUGGESTED BY THE SHAPES YOU CHOOSE:

A CIRCLE IS FAIRLY NONCOMMITTAL...

...COMPARED TO OTHER SHAPES:

AND THIS:

IS NOT THE SAME AS THIS:

SHOW RELATIONSHIPS

SOME STUFF IN COMMON

CHILD INHERITS SOME ATTRIBUTES OF PARENT

 CONNECTED!

ADD VISUAL REFINEMENTS

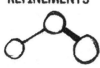

DISTORTION

RELATIVE SIZE

OVERLAP

Here's a handy phrase to remember the elements common to all kinds of visual models: "Things arranged into territories." Why?

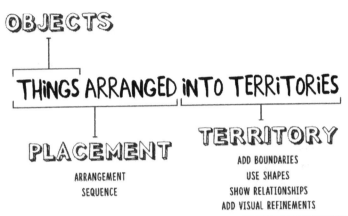

OBJECTS

THINGS ARRANGED INTO TERRITORIES

PLACEMENT
ARRANGEMENT
SEQUENCE

TERRITORY
ADD BOUNDARIES
USE SHAPES
SHOW RELATIONSHIPS
ADD VISUAL REFINEMENTS

TEST YOURSELF! | How many elements can you spot in this visual model?

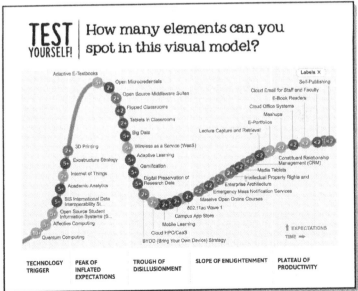

GIORGIA LUPI ON DRAWING DATA

Information designer. Cofounder and design director at @accuratstudio. Coauthor of Dear Data

For many, the word 'data-visualization' is associated with heavy programming skills, complex software and huge numbers. Believe it or not, lots of data visualization designers use old-fashioned sketching and drawing techniques on paper as their primary design tool.

In the first phase of data exploration, I am interested in the organization of the information, i.e. the kind of topics we are investigating, the correlations and the number of elements we are working with. I rarely use real data here, I am just giving shape to first visual possibilities about the 'architecture' of the visualization while having the data in mind.

In those phases, drawing with data can help raise new questions about the data itself.

In designing data visualizations, a very common approach is to start from the tools you have. This can lead you to adopt the easiest—but maybe not the best— solution to represent important aspects of the information.

As opposite, when I am sketching to explore the dimensions of a data set, I don't have access to the actual data with my pen and paper, but only to its logical organizations. This is an invaluable asset to help me focus on the meaning of information and not on numbers out of context.

Drawing is a primary form of understanding reality and expressing thoughts and ideas. Drawing, in any practice, helps you freely navigate possibilities and to visually think without limitations and boundaries. It allows connections to be made, it opens mental spaces.

And drawing also helps you to discover something you probably don't have in mind yet.

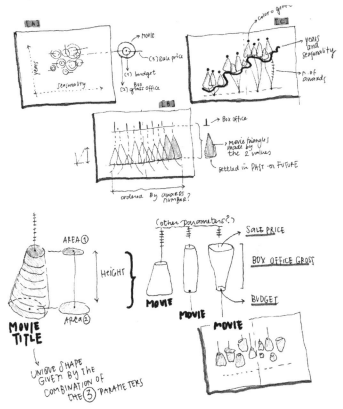

Explorations for "Selling at Sundance."

DAVE GRAY ON VISUAL THINKING

Dave Gray is the Founder of XPLANE, a visual thinking company, and author of GameStorming, the Connected Company and Liminal Thinking.

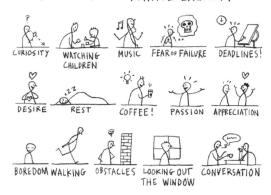

WHAT IGNITES CREATIVE ENERGY?

CURIOSITY · WATCHING CHILDREN · MUSIC · FEAR OF FAILURE · DEADLINES! · DESIRE · REST · COFFEE! · PASSION · APPRECIATION · BOREDOM · WALKING · OBSTACLES · LOOKING OUT THE WINDOW · CONVERSATION

Since childhood, I have always had a habit of drawing to understand new ideas. My teachers looked on this as everything from a mild distraction to downright disruptive. Sometimes they forbid me from drawing in class. But it was so core to me, so essential to my learning process, that I did it whenever I could.

I learned, though, that my drawings were often wrong. One day when I showed one of my drawings to my teacher after class and asked if I had understood it correctly. She told me my drawing was wrong, and that I had misunderstood. But at that point something magic happened: she picked up my pencil and started to correct my drawing, and I started to understand."

CULTURE   CULT

I learned a few things that day. First, learning works best when it is not a one-way thing. One person doesn't just pour knowledge into another person's head, like you pour tea into a teacup. It's a dialogue. Second, I learned that I could teach people how to teach me. By making a rough sketch of an idea, I could create a picture that functioned as a learning space where knowledge, and insights could be co-created with other people."

I vowed to make this co-creation a regular part of my learning process, and in doing so I soon learned that I was wrong far more often than I had realized.

But the learning method that I had discovered was so powerful that it became the foundation of my life and work. And when I was ready to start a company, it became the foundation of that too."

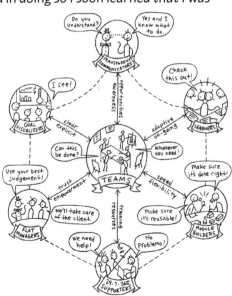

HOLD A VISUAL MEETING

Meetings are boring. Blah blah blah. Meetings are frustrating. People keep misunderstanding each other.

That's because words are not enough. Using paper and walls and **drawing**, we can make it better.

If your teammates are shy about drawing, you can hire a graphic facilitator to visualize the meeting as you have it (or you can do it!.)

And no one is shy about writing Post-its. It's an easy way to edge into working more visually. Post-its are modular, letting you use the wall to think spatially.

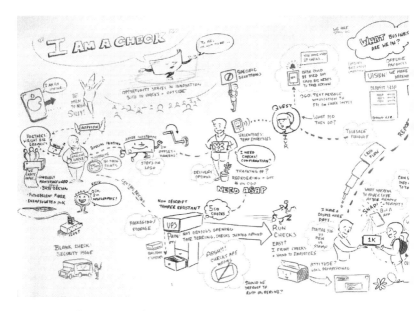

JAMES YOUNG

Partner at Tangible UX

James likes to hire a graphic facilitator for important client workshops. Graphic facilitators sketchnote the meeting's big ideas as they happen.

Here are two reasons why visual listening is a key element of the workshop:

1. It helps participants be present in the moment, as they don't have to worry about documenting anything.

2. It serves as an "artifact" that can be referenced during and after the workshop.

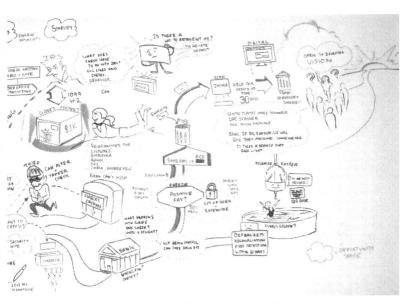

When I use graphical facilitators in meetings it helps everyone be on the same page as to what is said and discussed. If there are contradictions or details that are overlooked, the graphical facilitator quickly identifies them and the group discusses them.

Because the documentation is visual and being done in the moment, it simplifies the gnarliest problem into something that is digestible for the whole team. We can put it up on the wall and come back to it to discuss components of the drawing.

By giving the team a holistic picture of the problem or system it allows the team to move to solutions faster in a way that words and PowerPoint presentations cannot.

Above: A recording of a meeting on the "Life of a Check" held at a financial company.

TECHNIQUES FOR VISUAL MEETINGS

First, you want to get your ideas out of your head and on to paper where you can see them. Try freelisting! Silently write down as many ideas as you can, one per Post-it.

Next, we want to find patterns in the ideas! Try grouping them into similar groups. This is called affinity grouping. Everyone should go at once, then take a look to see what's out of place.

Finally, you can try mapping your ideas to a canvas. A canvas is like a visual worksheet you fill out with Post-it notes.

CANVASES SHAPE THINKING

Canvases were pioneered by Dave Sibbet at his company The Grove. This is his planning template from his book, *Visual Meetings*.

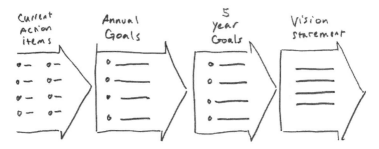

PLANNING TEMPLATE

Current Action items — Annual Goals — 5 year Goals — Vision statement

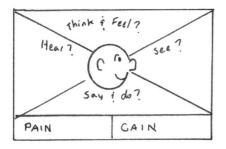

The Empathy Map is a canvas.

The best known Canvas is probably the Business Model Canvas (explained on page 158)

PUT THE TECHNIQUES TOGETHER AND HOLD A DESIGN CHARETTE

A charette is a short intense period of collaborative creation. Nowadays it's often called a design sprint, but I like the old name.

Let's pretend we're making a new product for travelers. We need some data to work with. We could freelist ideas about what people like and hate about travel. Or we can take user research and fragment it onto Post-its. One insight per Post-it!

Next, let's use our new found skill of affinity grouping to find the patterns in the data.

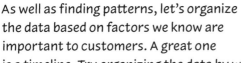

As well as finding patterns, let's organize the data based on factors we know are important to customers. A great one is a timeline. Try organizing the data by when it happens. For

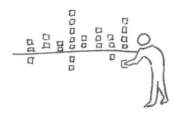

example, when traveling, first you plan. Then you pack. Then you go. If something happens more than once on the timeline, make a copy.

Another classic organizing principle is the 2x2 matrix.

My favorite 2x2 for designing start-ups is a frequency/ passion matrix. Go through your research, find all the things people care about when traveling and write them on post-its. Eating! Exchange rates! Language! Suitcases! Quiet hotels!

Place the issues on the matrix. We eat three times a day, but book a flight once. We sleep every night, but break a heel... maybe?

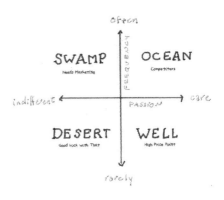

If the issue happens often and people care about it (like eating), it might be a problem worth building a business around.

Next you can map your data to some useful canvases. We could use the empathy map, from the previous page. Or we could try out one of Alex Osterwalder and Yves Pigneur's canvases.

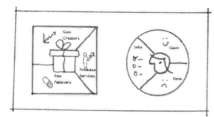

Use this canvas from Alex and Yves's book *Value Proposition Design* to understand what the right products and services are for your customers.

Next, draw a Storyboard ("Customer's Journey Storyboard" on page 96) showing the customer receiving the value.

Sometimes it's hard for introverts to contribute to brainstorms. Working silently when you freelist or draw can really help. You'll get more and better ideas!

In my classes our motto is: Generate apart, Evaluate together.

Next, we'll figure out how the product works! Draw a wireflow (page 123.) Draw your vision for the product silently and

separately first. Then share and combine ideas.

The schedule for drawing exercises are:

1. **DRAW**: 10 minutes

2. **EXPLAIN**: 1 minute each

3. **VOTE** on which drawing you want to build on (you can steal good ideas from anyone, but it's good to have a common base)

4. **DRAW AGAIN**, either a revision of the last idea or a new one—like designing the packaging or the landing page.

Make a wireframe (page 96) of the page where customers learn about how great your product is!

Finally let's take that value proposition and explain it to customers! Show potential customers tidy versions of:

* Your elevator pitch
* Your storyboard
* Your wireflows
* Your wireframe of a landing page or package.

These drawings help potential customers understand what you plan to make. Give the customers time to ask questions, or correct you on your assumptions.

Then show them the roadmap of features you plan to build. Let them swap the features they want with those they don't.

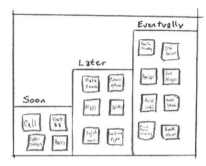

On the left are the features you plan to build first. In the middle the ones you expect people will want. On the right, crazy stuff one team member dreams of making someday!

Run this exercise with five to ten representatives of each market segment. Listen to what they say about the features. You can learn about what they really care about before you choose what to build.

Finally, it's time to use the Business Model Canvas to figure out how we'll make money.

The business model canvas is composed of nine regions, organized by how they affect each other. The right side of the canvas is outward looking, toward the customer. The left is inward looking, toward the company.

The customer is connected to the company's value proposition by channels (how we get the customer) and relationships (how we keep the customer,) which results in revenue.

The value proposition is realized by the company, composed of activities (hires), resources (materials and services) and partnerships. This results in costs. If costs are less than revenue, you have a viable business.

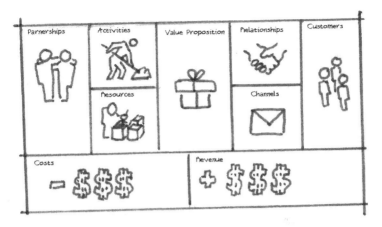

"Never write on the BMC. That's why God gave us Post-its."
—Alex Osterwalder.

Noam Zomerfeld, creating a Business Model Canvas in my Creative Entrepreneur class.

ALEX OSTERWALDER ON WHY HE WORKS VISUALLY.

Author of "Business Model Generation" and Founder of Strategyzer, Alex co-wrote the best-selling Business Model Generation *with Yves Pigneur (and 470 practitioners from 45 counties.) While most business books are just text, Alex and Yves wanted theirs to have photos and diagrams. They had to self-publish the first edition in order to realize their vision.*

Visuals help simplify and explain the complex in a way that words will never be able to. To understand something I need to understand the pieces and how they relate to each other. I can't do that in my head, so I use sticky notes and visuals to turn the abstract into something visual, visible, and tangible.

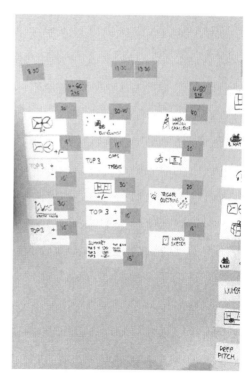

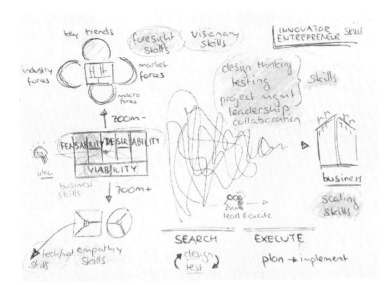

For example, when I design a workshop, write a book or text, or define our company's strategy, I use sticky notes and visuals to structure the ideas in my head. I do a brain dump by creating an individual sticky note for everything I can think of

related to the challenge I'm facing. Then I put them all on a large wall and cluster them until a structure emerges. That's how I make sense of any type of challenge I'm facing.

The wall is my desk.

DAN ROAM

Author of Back of the Napkin, Show and Tell *and* Draw to Win, *Dan Roam has built a career in teaching executives to express themselves more clearly using drawings.*

What is the simplest way to see if a leadership team is up-to-speed, on the same page, and in possession of an achievable vision? Ask them to draw."

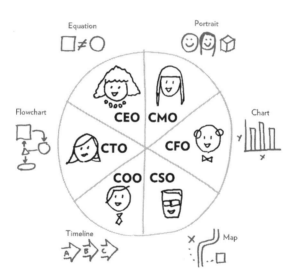

Over the past twenty-five years, I've worked with executive teams around the world. The scariest lesson is how often teams that thought they knew what they were thinking realize they really don't have a clear idea what each other just said.

A solution? Ask each member of the team to contribute the **just one picture** that best illustrates their individual contribution to the team and the organization.

The Chief Executive Officer draws the Visual Equation.

I'm the **CEO**.
Let me show you WHY we're doing what we're doing.
(I draw the Equation.)

As the leader of the organization, all eyes fall turn to the CEO whenever anything happens—good or bad. The best way the CEO can show *why* she has made the decisions she has is by showing a simple "visual equation."

Think of this as the moral of the story made visual; the simplest possible visual that says the most in the clearest possible way."

The Chief Marketing Officer draws the Portrait.

If there is anybody in the organization who better know **who** our audiences are and **what** we are offering them, it's the CMO. (How can we market if we don't know to whom? Or what we're trying to tell them?)"

I'm the **CMO**.
Let me show you WHO our customers are wnd WHAT we offer them.
(I draw the Portrait.)

When the CMO needs to say "we are doing **this** for **these people**," nothing beats a simple, iconic portrait illustrating the who and the what.

The Chief Financial Officer draws the Chart.

I'm the **CFO**.
Let me show you HOW MUCH we have and how much we need.
(I draw the Chart.)

Who owns the top line, the bottom line, and every line in-between? The CFO does. So when Wall Street or the investors comes knocking, it's time for the CFO to share the charts. How much? This much. What are the financial trends? These lines.

If the CEO can't show the numbers in a way that makes sense, how can we be sure he knows them himself?

The Chief Strategy Officer draws the Map.

It is the job of the CSO to sketch out the opportunity landscape, plot in the competitions' positions, and map in the right moves. That requires a map. The CSO better be able to draw it.

I'm the **CSO**.
Let me show you WHERE we are now and where we are going.
(I draw the Map.)

It is also the CSO's job to make sure everyone else sees where those moves are going to take the organization —so that map better be clear, readable—and show the mine fields."

The Chief Operations Officer draws the Timeline.

Only 60% of Fortune 500 companies have a COO, but that number is rising again. Why? Because getting everything done in sequence and on time is only getting harder.

That's why the COO' best friend is the timeline: the single picture that shows what needs to get done, who is doing it, and most important: in what order.

I'm the **COO**.
Let me show you WHEN we are taking each step along the way.
(I draw the Timeline.)

I'm the **CTO**.
Let me show you HOW we are technologically making this all happen.
(I draw the Flowchart.)

The Chief Technical Officer draws the Flowchart.

The vision is clear, the numbers are there, and the process is mapped. What remains? Building the systems and architecture that makes it technologically feasible. That's the job of the CTO.

The picture she draws? The flowchart; it shows how the pieces interact, how the information flows, and how to monitor all the incoming data. It's usually the most complex picture, so demands unusual attention to clarity.

The pictures don't need to be elaborate, don't need to be polished, and don't need to be perfect. But they do need to be created, they do need to be shared, and they absolutely need to be seen.

DRAW ALL THE THINGS

 Don't forget! Drawing isn't just some creative thing artist people do. It's a way to make ideas tangible, to get the stuff in our head out so we can figure out what to do with it.

The world has gotten so complicated. Work is full of reports and analyses and emails and it's hard to make sense of it all, much less make anything new and useful.

We need ways to make work make sense. Drawing is my favorite. Not just because it's effective, but because it's fun too. We spend at least eight hours a day at work. Shouldn't we enjoy it?

Draw every day. Make better stuff. Make sense of all the crazy. Celebrate the wonderous.

Be happy.

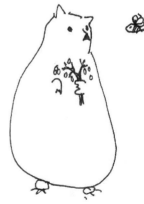

BOOKS I READ
AND YOU SHOULD TOO

Berinato, Scott. *Good Charts: The HBR Guide to Making Smarter, More Persuasive Data Visualizations.* Harvard Business Review, 2016.

Brown, Sunni. *Doodle Revolution: Unlock the Power to Think Differently.* Portfolio Penguin, 2015.

Brunetti, Ivan. *Cartooning: Philosophy and Practice.* Yale UP, 2011.

Crowe, Norman, and Paul Laseau. *Visual Notes for Architects and Designers.* Wiley, 2012.

Edwards, Betty. *Drawing on the Right Side of the Brain.* Tarcher/Penguin, 2012.

Kliment, Stephen A. *Architectural Sketching and Rendering: Techniques for Designers and Artists.* Whitney Library of Design, 1984.

Nicolaïdes, Kimon. *The Natural Way to Draw: A Working Plan for Art Study.* Morison Press, 2013.

Roam, Dan. *The Back of the Napkin: Solving Problems and Selling Ideas with Pictures.* Portfolio/Penguin, 2013.

Rohde, Mike. *The Sketchnote Handbook: The Illustrated Guide to Visual Note Taking.* Peachpit, 2013.

Seddon, Tony. *Draw Your Own Alphabets: Thirty Fonts to Scribble, Sketch, & Make Your Own.* Princeton Architectural, 2013.

WEBSITES & COMMUNITIES

Urban Sketchers community: http://www.urbansketchers.org

Sketchnote Army http://sketchnotearmy.com/

The work of Kate Rutter http://intelleto.com/

The work of Danny Gregory: http://www.dannygregory.com

The work of Wendy McNaughton: http://wendymacnaughton.com

The Work of Dave Gray: http://www.xplaner.com/

Pencil Me In

I love teaching drawing to help people answer hard questions.

For updates and more exercises, visit pencilmeinthebook.com